NSA SEMINARS
An Introduction to Buddhism

by

George M. Williams

World Tribune Press

This book is dedicated to Daisaku Ikeda, president of the Soka Gakkai International, in appreciation for his unwavering efforts in the cause of world peace.

Table of Contents

Preface

I am very pleased that we have been able to publish a revised edition of *NSA Seminars*. This book represents one small aspect of our ongoing efforts to introduce the Buddhism of Nichiren Daishonin to people everywhere who are seeking peace, happiness and a more meaningful way of life.

I am also pleased that we have been able to publish this revised edition to coincide with the auspicious occasion of the thirtieth anniversary of the Kosen-rufu Day Ceremony held in Japan on March 16, 1958. On that occasion, some 6,000 youthful believers gathered at the Nichiren Shoshu head temple, Taiseki-ji, with Josei Toda, second president of the Soka Gakkai. Only days away from his own demise and thus the completion of his mission, President Toda passed on the baton of the lay Buddhist movement to his youthful followers, led by Daisaku Ikeda. Mr. Ikeda later became the third Soka Gakkai President, and in 1975, the first Soka Gakkai International President, in recognition of the worldwide spread of the movement.

In recent years, the number of Americans who have come to embrace the Daishonin's Buddhism has risen sharply, as more and more people have discovered the truth of this teaching. But what is this truth?

SGI President Ikeda himself once explained that the fundamental solution to all of life's problems—economic, social, political, educational, and of course, personal—can be found within the individual. He stated, as an overview of the purpose of Buddhism:

Buddhism elucidates the two basic aspects inherent in human life as fundamental darkness and ultimate enlightenment. Fundamental darkness activates one's evil nature and unhappiness in life, while ultimate enlightenment does the same for the power of good and happiness. Buddhism terms the roots of human distrust, hatred and fear as fundamental darkness. I would like to emphasize that, ultimately speaking, we are now facing an age which requires a revolution of life; this implies that we cannot discuss peace or culture in their true sense if we neglect the necessity of the assiduous practice of faith in the higher teachings of Buddhism to awaken the wisdom within each individual to live humanistically in peace and happiness. In other words, I would like to emphasize that this faith enables the transformation of fundamental darkness into ultimate enlightenment.

Nichiren Daishonin, who lived 700 years ago in Japan, taught a specific and universally feasible way of Buddhist practice to manifest the ultimate enlightenment latent in each individual. He held that, to be considered valid, a religious doctrine must be able to show three kinds of proof: documentary, theoretical and actual. That is, it must possess a legitimate body of scripture, be logically consistent, and most important, enable everyone who practices it to overcome suffering and live happily in this world. One who begins the practice of Nichiren Daishonin's Buddhism will soon find that it possesses all three. Reading the teachings, he will discover that they make sense; motivated to try the practice, he will discover the truth of these teachings within himself.

As Nichiren Daishonin's Buddhism continues to spread across the globe, the Soka Gakkai International now has members in almost 120 nations. This is truly a remarkable achievement, and a remarkable testimony to the power of his Buddhism itself.

Now, as we in NSA look forward to 1990, when we will celebrate three important anniversaries—the 700th anniversary of the founding of the head temple, Taiseki-ji, the 60th anniversary of the founding of the Soka Gakkai, and the 30th anniversary of the founding of NSA here in the United States—we hope that still more people will learn of Nichiren Daishonin's Buddhism and discover its truth through the three proofs. Toward this end, we have revised and reissued this volume. If this book helps the reader to gain even a little deeper understanding of true Buddhism, thereby opening greater vistas to personal happiness, I myself will be very happy indeed.

GEORGE M. WILLIAMS
General Director, NSA
March 16, 1988

1
A Brief Buddhist History

Shakyamuni and the Roots of the Religion

Buddhism derives from the teachings of a man called Shakya-muni (also known as Gautama or Siddhartha), the historical Buddha who lived nearly 3,000 years ago. According to tradition, he was heir to the throne of a kingdom in northern India and excelled early in the civil and military arts.

Though raised amid the luxury of a royal palace, he found himself unable to enjoy its pleasures. He was troubled by the realization that all human beings, regardless of their station, are subject to the laws of impermanence and must undergo the universal sufferings of birth, aging, illness and death. At nineteen (some sources say twenty-nine), Shakyamuni left the palace to lead the life of a religious ascetic in search of answers to the problem of human suffering.

He studied under prominent religious teachers of his day, but dissatisfied with the results of their disciplines, he embarked on a solitary practice. He is said to have nearly died from severe fasts and other austerities he imposed upon himself. Finally sensing the futility of these exercises, he sat in meditation beneath a pipal tree near Buddh Gaya and there attained enlightenment.

Buddhism is unusual among the major religions in that it makes no claim to divine revelation. Shakyamuni achieved enlightenment through his own efforts. The main stream of Buddhist thought consequently denies any "higher reality" apart from daily life, and finds all possibilities within the human being.

What was the enlightenment Shakyamuni attained? This is a difficult question, impossible to answer simply. The very notion of Buddhist practice derives from the premise that enlightenment is not an abstract truth to be grasped intellectually, but a condition of human life acquired through personal effort. Scriptural accounts and commentaries say that Shakyamuni awoke to the eternity of his own life and perceived the law of causality operating throughout past, present and future.

This concept or law of causation explains the fundamental process whereby all phenomena and sentient beings in the universe occur or exist as the result of causes. Buddhism calls this *karma* and says that all things in the universe are subject to this law of cause and effect. Consequently, nothing can exist independently of other things or arise of its own accord. For this reason the theory of causation is often referred to as "the essential interdependence of things." Because this web of causation that binds all things is temporal as well as spatial, not only are all things in existence at the present moment dependent upon one another, but all things existing in the past and future are as well.

Shakyamuni realized all this from the depths of his life. It was far more than a mere intellectual or spiritual awakening; it was a total life experience that changed his very being. From this point on he sought to teach that people suffer because of ignorance—ignorance not of factual knowledge but of the true nature of life.

The culmination of Shakyamuni's fifty-year teaching is found in the Lotus Sutra, that teaching he is said to have expounded in the last eight years of his life. This sutra reveals that the ultimate and final purpose of all his many previous teachings was to lead all people to Buddhahood. It states, "At the start I pledged to make all people perfectly equal to me, without any distinction between us."

The Lotus Sutra declares that all human beings have the potential for Buddhahood, and the Buddha himself is an ordinary human being. The sutra's recognition of the fundamental equality of all people by virtue of their innate Buddha nature characterizes the highest Buddhist thinking.

After Shakyamuni's death, his followers convened the First Council to compile his teachings and commit them to memory. Tradition has it that subsequent councils were called in later centuries to submit the Buddhist canon to a process of review and standardization. These teachings, organized in a form that could be memorized and recited, are called sutras. They were transmitted orally for some time; some scholars surmise that not until the first century A.D. were they set down in writing.

Because Shakyamuni taught for so long at so many levels it was perhaps inevitable that varying interpretations would arise, eventually leading to the formation of schools. In time, two distinct streams of Buddhism emerged. The first is called Theravada ("School of the Elders") or Hinayana ("Lesser Vehicle"—so dubbed by its detractors). This Buddhism is based on Shakyamuni's earlier teachings and stresses the denial of desire, renunciation of the world, and strict adherence to monastic precepts and to the letter of Buddhist scripture in search of personal salvation. This form of Buddhism spread south into Ceylon and Southeast Asia.

The second stream of Buddhism is called Mahayana ("Greater Vehicle") and aims not only at personal salvation, but enlightenment for all. Mahayana emphasizes practice in the mundane world for the sake of all human beings, and adherence to the spirit, rather than the letter, of Buddhist canon. Mahayana spread north over the Silk Road to China and from there to Korea and Japan.

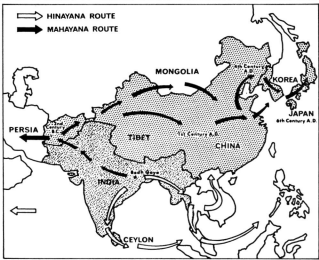

The spread of Buddhism after Shakyamuni.

The Theravada teachings were among the first to be compiled, as they centered around precepts which were needed to regulate monastic communities. Later, as Buddhism spread more widely among the lay community, the Mahayana teachings, including the Lotus Sutra, were compiled.

Theravada in time became increasingly removed from the lay community and intent upon fine points of doctrinal investigation, and lost its vitality as a religious force. Mahayana, geared toward vigorous dissemination of the teachings and salvation for all, gradually gained momentum and emerged as a new religious movement.

Buddhism was probably introduced to China sometime before the birth of Christ, and several centuries' effort at translation and study were begun. It was in China that Buddhism was systematized. Chih-i, also called T'ien-t'ai, a brilliant scholar of the sixth century, organized the entire body of sutras into a coherent philosophical system.

Both the Lotus Sutra and the Buddhism of T'ien-t'ai, which derived from it, speak of a true entity of fundamental law permeating all things. Both assert that all people can become Buddhas. But for the most part, this remained a theoretical proposition. Practice involved hours of daily meditation, and the subtleties of doctrine barred this form of Buddhism from all but the most learned. In theory it was universal; in practice it remained largely the province of the clergy and the nobility.

Soon after T'ien-t'ai's death, Japanese scholars traveled to China to bring his teachings back to their homeland. Among these scholars was Saicho, later known as Dengyo. He brought this highest development of Buddhism by T'ien-t'ai back to Japan and established a center of learning at Mt. Hiei. He was responsible for a religious revolution that brought about a period of prosperity and highly sophisticated culture in the Heian period.

By the thirteenth century, Buddhism, now centered in Japan, had passed the zenith of its prosperity and, aided by natural disaster and social upheaval, entered a state of decline. Priests of opposing temples armed themselves, joined only by a common departure from the original Buddhist spirit.

The Shingon Sect, for example, incorporated a heavy element of ritual and mysticism to appeal to the aristocracy. The Jodo Sect offered deferred hopes to the suffering masses with promises of rebirth in the Pure Land. Buddhism had become a religion of escape.

Nichiren Daishonin and his true Buddhism

Into this rather confused state of religious affairs, Nichiren Daishonin was born on February 16, 1222 in a small fishing village on the eastern coast of Japan. As a young boy, he entered a temple near his home in order to receive an education, since the only schools at that time were the temples themselves. Eventually he entered the priesthood.

The young priest studied the sutras of Shakyamuni and wondered why so many different teachings had all come from the ideas of one sage. He was also troubled by the fact that no existing form of Buddhism had been able to truly help people find happiness in their daily lives—the one goal to which Shakyamuni had been committed.

With these questions in mind, Nichiren Daishonin set out to study all existing Buddhist thought. For sixteen years he traveled throughout Japan, studying at the highest centers of learning. As he studied he was especially concerned about the bewildering multiplicity of Buddhist sects and the doctrinal contradictions within the Buddhist canon. He was convinced that there must be one among the many sutras that represented the highest truth. He read all of the sutras and reviewed the teachings of T'ien-t'ai. Consequently, he came to the conclusion that the Lotus Sutra was the highest sutra and that its title, *Myoho-renge-kyo*, contained the entire essence of the sutra.

Very early in the morning of April 28, 1253, at Seicho-ji—the temple where he had begun his studies—the Daishonin chanted Nam-myoho-renge-kyo publicly for the first time. In doing this, he established a universal practice, opening the way to Buddhahood for all people. It was a practice so wondrously simple that anyone could do it, and yet so profound that it could unlock an infinite, enlightened wisdom in any individual. What he did, in essence, was enable the ordinary person to actualize in himself the reality described by centuries of Buddhist philosophy.

Throughout the Daishonin's life, he refused to compromise in pointing out doctrinal errors and corruption in the religious world. This won him many enemies among both clerical and civil authorities, and he endured persecution throughout much of his life, including two exiles and an attempted execution. Nevertheless, he was able to solidify the foundation of his teaching for the generations to come through his indefatigable efforts at teaching his followers and writing down all the tenets of his true Buddhism. Ultimately, on October 12, 1279, he inscribed the true object of worship known as the Dai-Gohonzon in order to assure that mankind would eternally have a focus for the chanting of Nam-myoho-renge-kyo.

The establishment of a universally accessible means of practice marked a radical departure from previous forms of Buddhism and in this sense, Nichiren Daishonin's teaching must be regarded as an entirely new religion, not merely an outgrowth of earlier forms.

His Buddhism was kept alive by a priesthood centered near Mt. Fuji for nearly 700 years. Then, when the post-World War II constitution brought freedom of religion to Japan, his followers were able to disseminate it freely. In recent years, Nichiren Shoshu ("orthodox school of Nichiren") has spread to more than ninety countries, becoming a world religion.

Nichiren Daishonin himself added little to the theory of Buddhism. His achievement lay in another dimension. What he did was establish a practice whereby anyone might transform what was previously abstract and ideal theory into a concrete and beautiful reality of daily life. By analogy, one might think of previous Buddhist teachings as reams and reams of the most exquisite music which virtually no one had ever heard—because there was no instrument to play it. Nichiren Daishonin provided an instrument, and for the first time the music would resonate within and still people's hearts. His contribution signaled a shift in the current of Buddhist history and a renaissance of the Buddhist spirit.

REFERENCES

Fundamentals of Buddhism. Y. Kirimura. Los Angeles: World Tribune Press, 1982.

Major Writings of Nichiren Daishonin, vol. 1. Edited and Translated by The Seikyo Times. Tokyo: Nichiren Shoshu International Center, 1979.

World Tribune: The Introductory Issue, "Buddhism: the Historical Perspective." Los Angeles: World Tribune Press, February 8, 1982.

Joy, confidence and vitality abound where NSA members gather to share true Buddhism.

A guest is warmly welcomed at a meeting.

2
Defining the Buddhist Faith

The Three Proofs of Religion

What is the measure of a religion? It would seem that man seeks religious teaching and practice in order to explain the unexplainable, to provide direction where there was previously aimlessness, or to give meaning and order to the seemingly random experience of life. Perhaps, when all is said and done, it could be simply stated that man seeks religion to provide him with happiness. Happiness is a rather vague, sometimes unpopular term—it can be spiritual, emotional or physical. It can stem from immediate gratification or long-range objectives. Whatever the case, it would be hard to argue against the fact that the human being spends most of his or her waking life striving toward some individually defined concept of happiness.

Buddhism is a religion taught for the human being by a human being we refer to as the Buddha. Because the Buddha is no more or less than human himself, he recognizes that what human beings seek most and what also motivates them most is their own happiness. Actually, the Buddha simply means "enlightened human being" and can refer to any number of individuals—from the man known as Shakyamuni, the first historical Buddha, to the man we call Nichiren Daishonin, whom Nichiren Shoshu considers to be the original and ultimate Buddha.

Thus, we come to the conclusion that the Buddhist faith has been revealed to allow human beings to seek their happiness. One problem, however, is that the concept of faith, by nature, embodies, to one extent or another, the concept of belief. Belief is a hard thing to adhere to in our times. Staggering changes are taking place in the human community and more and more people are questioning what were, until now, commonly accepted attitudes about life. Change has affected every facet of our daily reality and our entire society has come to reconsider its direction. At the same time, all of us continue to live under the spectre of imminent destruction posed by nuclear weapons and attendant barbaric concepts such as "winnable nuclear war." It is no wonder that ours is an age of skepticism and doubt.

Any religion that avoids proving its doctrine, theory and practice would seek to deny the questioning nature of man. Buddhism suggests that we evaluate religion according to the "three proofs" *(sansho)*. These offer a standard for gauging the quality and validity of a religion. They are known as documentary, theoretical and actual proof.

In the pages that follow we will examine Nichiren Shoshu Buddhism from these three criteria. First, we will address the documented ideals of the religion—the historical Lotus Sutra which provides much of Nichiren Shoshu's theoretical underpinning and Nichiren Daishonin's *Gosho* (writings) which spell out the specifics of the practice and the objectives of the Buddhist faith. Second, we will examine the theories of life expounded by Buddhism, attempting to highlight the common-sense and rational approach of these theories as being consistent with the Buddhist notion of religious faith.

Finally, and most importantly, we will spell out the way in which stated doctrine and theory in Nichiren Shoshu are implemented as a real process in everyday human existence—a process that leads to the creation of actual proof as a result of adherence to the doctrinal and theoretical tenets of faith.

It is in its insistence upon actual proof that Nichiren Shoshu reveals its greatness. Nichiren Daishonin himself said, "I, Nichiren, conclude from my own experiences in Buddhism that literal and theoretical proofs are vital factors to judge religions, but actual proof is far superior to both." The elements of religious practice and their results deserve more attention than they are generally given. Naturally, results must substantiate theory.

Science is highly respected because it backs up its ideas with experimentation. For a theory to be considered valid, experiments must offer the same proof no matter how many times or under what conditions they may be repeated. Natural sciences such as physics and chemistry go to great lengths to produce substantial evidence.

It is clear that a religion—because it is essentially a matter of faith—is something that can never be proven by scientific experimentation. Nevertheless, if a religion that purports to explain life cannot at least equal the *effort* of science to demonstrate continuing and overwhelming proof to its believers in daily usage, it is of little worth. The proof of Nichiren Shoshu lies in the undeniable enlightenment that becomes the indestructible possession of each and every lifetime-practicing member. The process of attaining this enlightenment is what we call human revolution—a process which comprises the underlying theme of all that follows.

The Documents of the Teaching

The believers of Nichiren Shoshu are fortunate in that the founder of the religion, Nichiren Daishonin, the man referred to as the original Buddha, left behind a quantity of letters and theses that have been compiled in a volume known as the *Gosho*. These writings include theoretical explanations as well as practical instructions concerning the Buddhist faith.

It should be noted that, prior to the formalization of his teachings, beginning on April 28, 1253, Nichiren Daishonin had engaged in almost two decades of exhaustive study and research. He aimed at eliminating the confusion of the Buddhist teachings that existed in his time and at pointing out a clear, new direction for the Buddhist faith in the future. Our Western religious tradition might cause us to wonder about this process; after all, should one tamper with explanations of the Law handed down from on high? In this context, what should be understood is that Buddhism has always been a religion which has evolved and changed in accordance with the people and the times. The Buddhist canon is not the creation of some deity—it is an explanation of the unchangeable Law of life that has been revealed by a succession of enlightened human beings we refer to as Buddhas.

In Nichiren Daishonin's time, the Buddhist Law, as had been predicted by Shakyamuni, was corrupted and vastly misinterpreted by great numbers of Buddhist believers—both priests and laity. As a youth, Nichiren Daishonin fully realized that it was his great mission to restore the purity of the Buddhist Law and make it practicable for the endless succession of generations to come. It was to this end that he engaged in almost twenty years of traveling from temple to temple throughout Japan, seeking out every available sutra in order to crystallize the essence of the Buddhist teaching.

The conclusion the Daishonin arrived at was that the Lotus Sutra represented the apex of all Buddhist thought. This sutra was to provide the Daishonin with the theoretical underpinning, or blueprint, which he would use as a reference in the exposition of his new true Buddhist teaching. In his *Gosho* there are many references to the Lotus Sutra and, prior to his death in 1282, Nichiren Daishonin gave lectures on the Lotus Sutra which were translated by his main disciple Nikko, and which exist today under the title of "A Record of the Oral Teachings" (*Ongi Kuden*).

It should be clearly understood that Nichiren Daishonin's teachings are not a derivative of the Lotus Sutra. Rather, he used this sutra as a theoretical reference for what he had to say; in this way, he could spend more time giving practical explanations of his teaching, avoiding redundant and abstract philosophizing. Because the Lotus Sutra is such a major influence in the teaching of Nichiren Shoshu, we would do well to examine the historical and philosophical context of this document with regard to the entire body of Buddhist sutras.

The Lotus Sutra

Of the numerous Buddhist scriptures, the Lotus Sutra has from ancient times been regarded as pre-eminent. It has been revered since antiquity as the sutra which Shakyamuni Buddha expounded in the last eight years of his life to accomplish the purpose of his advent in this world.

The Lotus Sutra consists of twenty-eight chapters. Doctrinally speaking, it can be divided into two parts—the first fourteen chapters and the latter fourteen chapters. The former half is known as the theoretical teaching and the latter half as the essential teaching.

The principal chapter in the theoretical teaching is the second (*Hoben*) chapter. In this chapter Shakyamuni reveals that he will finally explain the true purpose of the provisional teachings with which he had led the people up until this point by revealing the true teaching. He further declares that belief in this true teaching will lead all people equally to Buddhahood. This statement is in great contrast to earlier teachings of Shakyamuni in which he had stated that certain people, because of their sex, life-condition, or whatever, could never attain Buddhahood. Therefore, the essential point of the second chapter of the Lotus Sutra is that Buddhahood is a possibility for every human being, no matter what his or her situation or condition may be.

The doctrine of the essential teaching is based on the sixteenth (*Juryo*) chapter. This chapter, together with the second chapter, comprises the core of the Lotus Sutra. The sixteenth chapter says that all people think that Shakyamuni Buddha attained enlightenment at Buddh Gaya in India; however, Shakyamuni reveals that he actually attained Buddhahood in the inconceivably remote past and he has been a Buddha ever since.

In explaining his life in this way, Shakyamuni is representing the eternal and universal Law of life underlying his teachings as an historical Buddha. Put more simply, whereas the second chapter of the Lotus Sutra admits to the possibility of all human beings attaining enlightenment to the Law of the universe, the sixteenth chapter explains that this enlightenment is in truth something that exists eternally within life. Therefore, attaining Buddhahood is not a matter of some future destination; rather, the correct practice of Buddhism allows us to inevitably reveal the enlightenment that eternally resides within.

The shortcoming of the Lotus Sutra is that, having explained this much and given so much hope to those who heard it, it never clarified precisely what the Law of the universe is or what the practice is that one must follow in order to realize it. The implication contained within the sutra itself is that the true, eternal Law will be revealed in some latter age when the theoretical teachings of Shakyamuni will have lost their power to help the people.

So, taking his cue from this sutra, Nichiren Daishonin realized that his was the age in which the Law was being lost and that it was his mission both to clarify the Law once and for all and to describe a practice that would enlighten all mankind to that Law—the ultimate objective of all Buddhas. It is in Nichiren Daishonin's *Gosho* that we find his complete revelation of the Law in addition to instructions as to how his teachings are to be carried out. For that reason, we now turn our attention to that most important document of the Nichiren Shoshu religion.

Fundamentals of the Practice

As mentioned previously, Nichiren Daishonin left behind more than 400 different writings—letters to his disciples and a variety of theses—which have been compiled into what is known as the *Gosho.* Within the pages of this text are contained not only the theoretical blueprints that underlie true Buddhism, but also detailed instructions as to the components of the Buddhist practice and directions as to how these components are to be utilized in everyday life.

Original manuscripts of letters and theses authored by Nichiren Daishonin have been preserved for 700 years.

Of utmost importance is the recognition that Nichiren Daishonin was far more than a man of theory and dogma. He was a
man of action who was adamant in his conviction that Buddhism is
a religion to be lived, not just believed in a spiritual or philosophical sense. His conviction led him to the conclusion that what was
needed to restore Buddhism in this day and age was a simple yet
profound practice that would be accessible to every living being.
The sutras of Shakyamuni, even the beautiful teachings of the
Lotus Sutra, could be little more than objects for speculation and
meditation.

For the common man, many of whom lacked the knowledge or
capacity for such things, an approach to the Buddhist faith based
only on the teachings of the sutras was impossible. The sutras
were written in an age when Buddhism was spread mainly among
the ruling class and intelligensia in hopes that its principles would
filter down to the masses. Nichiren Daishonin understood that
the coming ages of man would require a practice that could be
utilized by every human being. Clarifying this practice became his
essential purpose. This purpose undergirds every writing in the
Gosho.

Basically, what the Daishonin postulated was that one should
chant a mantra to an object of worship inscribed in mandala-like
form. In addition, he prescribed faith, practice and study as being
the three processes by which Buddhism moves from the world of
abstract theory into the reality of everyday existence. Let us now
take a look at these fundamentals of the true Buddhist religion.

The Prayer

On April 28, 1253, Nichiren Daishonin first publicly proclaimed
that the essence of his teaching lay in chanting the mantra, Nam-
myoho-renge-kyo. *Myoho-renge-kyo* is a Japanese pronunciation of
the Chinese title of the Lotus Sutra and *nam* is a Sanskrit word
meaning devotion, which the Daishonin added to complete the
chant, also referred to as *daimoku.*

The Daishonin explained his premise by giving this rationale in a writing referred to, appropriately enough, as "The One Essential Phrase":

Since the Lotus Sutra defines our life as the Buddha's life, our mind as the Buddha's wisdom and our actions as the Buddha's behavior, all who embrace and believe in even a single phrase or verse of this sutra will be endowed with these three properties. Nam-myoho-renge-kyo is only one phrase, but it contains the essence of the entire sutra. . .

Everything has its essential point, and the heart of the Lotus Sutra is its title, Nam-myoho-renge-kyo. Truly, if you chant this in the morning and evening, you are correctly reading the entire Lotus Sutra. Chanting daimoku twice is the same as reading the entire sutra twice, one hundred daimoku equal one hundred readings of the sutra, and a thousand daimoku, a thousand readings of the sutra. Thus, if you ceaselessly chant daimoku, you will be continually reading the Lotus Sutra.

What does Nam-myoho-renge-kyo mean? Nichiren Daishonin stated that it is the essential reality of life. This implies that the phrase cannot be understood by verbal definition alone. Indeed, the practice of Buddhism is the only thing which can ultimately reveal the deepest meanings of Nam-myoho-renge-kyo. Nevertheless, there is a superficial definition for each of the component words.

As mentioned previously, *nam* derives from Sanskrit and means dedication, or the perfect relation of one's own life with eternal truth. Strangely, the word "religion," which derives from Latin, originally meant "to bind strongly to something" and so is also encompassed by the word *nam*. The significance of *nam* is actually twofold. One is, as just mentioned, to dedicate one's own life to or become one with the eternal truth of life. The other is to draw infinite energy from this source and take positive action toward relieving the suffering of others.

What is this eternal truth? It is *Myoho-renge-kyo*, the title of the Lotus Sutra. *Myoho* literally means the Mystic Law. *Myo* (mystic) signifies "unfathomable," and *ho* means "law." *Myoho* is the incomprehensible law which permeates all the realities of life.

Buddhism postulates that all existence at one time or another assumes a physical condition with shape, size and kinetic energy. At other times existence may be incorporeal (in a state known as *ku* in Buddhism). No matter how reality may appear or change, its fundamental essence is eternal. Phenomena (*ho*) are changeable, but pervading all phenomena is the constant entity called *myo*.

Renge literally means lotus flower. Buddhism uses the lotus to explain the profound law of causality because the lotus produces its flowers and seeds at the same time. The lotus is therefore the symbol of simultaneous cause and effect (*inga guji*). Simultaneous cause and effect means that in truth our future is determined by present causes, even though we generally perceive causes and effects to be separated by time (*inga iji*). Thus the law of cause and effect is also a principle of personal responsibility for one's own destiny, or karma. However, because the innermost depth of our life—the eternal core of Nam-myoho-renge-kyo—remains independent of the karmic cycle we have created through our past deeds, we can transform our karma by tapping this core and thereby create absolute happiness. This is also represented by another quality of the lotus. Its beautiful blossoms spring forth from a muddy swamp, yet they are unsoiled by the mud. In other words, the innermost nature of our life remains untainted despite the bad karma we may have created. *Renge* thus means to reveal the most fundamental nature of the reality of life.

Finally, *kyo* indicates sutras, or the teachings of the Buddha. In a broader sense, it includes the activities of all living beings and phenomena throughout the universe. By tapping the Mystic Law within, each person can experience this universal harmony in his or her daily life. The Chinese character for *kyo* also means the warp of cloth, symbolizing the continuity of life throughout the past, present and future—the eternal, recurring nature of life.

The Object of Worship

Nichiren Daishonin established an object of worship known as the Gohonzon. This is in the form of a mandala inscribed with Chinese characters. The Gohonzon is generally inscribed on either wood or paper by the high priest of the sect, depending on where and by whom it is to be used. All members of Nichiren Shoshu have a Gohonzon in their homes.

On the Gohonzon itself are inscribed the Chinese characters for "Nam-myoho-renge-kyo" and "Nichiren." The Gohonzon is thus considered a physical object which embodies a perfect fusion of the Law and the Person. To the left and right of these characters, which are written down the center of the Gohonzon, are inscribed names of different historical and mythical characters which represent the different life-conditions known as the Ten Worlds (see "Buddhist Theory").

The question might be raised as to the need for an external object of worship, particularly in the form of a paper scroll covered with Chinese characters. Buddhist theory is quite clear in explaining that the infinite power of the universe exists within each human life. In addition, in his own writings, Nichiren Daishonin said, "Never seek this Gohonzon outside yourself." Why, therefore, is an object of worship necessary?

Perhaps the simplest way to answer would be to ask the reader of these lines to begin laughing—right now. Unless one were to find something hilarious in these few paragraphs, such a request would be impossible to fulfill. The reason is simple: nothing to be read here is particularly funny.

Now, Buddhism postulates that each human being has the nature of enlightenment within. How to bring it out is the question. One might want it to come out, but without an actual connection being made between one's life and the environment, the life-condition of enlightenment is impossible to manifest. No one operates in a vacuum. It is our interaction with the world around us that provides the dynamics and meaning of life.

We need an environmental connection to bring out our laughter, anger or whatever. Similarly, a connection is needed to bring out the Buddha nature of enlightenment. Nichiren Daishonin inscribed the Gohonzon as the proper object to bring out this deepest condition of our existence.

True Buddhism teaches that the Gohonzon manifests the life of Nichiren Daishonin, a life fully enlightened to Nam-myoho-renge-kyo. This same Nam-myoho-renge-kyo exists dormant within each human being. When a person chants to the Gohonzon, a fusion is achieved and the life-condition of enlightenment wells up from within. The Gohonzon is not some external deity, bestowing that which the believer does not already possess. Rather, it is an environmental stimulus that allows each person to manifest his or her ultimate human potential, creating an unshakable happiness in the midst of an ever-changing reality.

The concept of the object of worship is perhaps one of the most difficult to fathom in the Buddhist religion. What should be understood is that Buddhism is something which always deals with the interrelation between the individual and his or her environment. In this sense, an environmental object of worship which serves as a catalyst for the creation of an indestructible life-condition is essential.

Faith, Practice and Study

In a writing entitled "The True Entity of Life," Nichiren Daishonin stated, "Exert yourself in the two ways of practice and study. Without practice and study there can be no Buddhism. You must not only persevere yourself, you must also teach others. Both practice and study arise from faith." In saying this, he set forth the three things which are considered to be the integral components of the Buddhist religion. Anyone who wishes to consider himself a Buddhist in the true sense of the word should strive to harmonize these three in the course of his daily life.

Faith in Buddhism has a somewhat different meaning than the traditional concepts usually generated by Judeo-Christian doctrine. In a religion which emphasizes the importance of actual proof, there is no way that faith can be construed as meaning blind belief. Faith in Buddhism is defined as a level of expectation. For the new member beginning to practice the Daishonin's true Buddhism, the expectation might be simply that the practice will lead to desired and promised results. Ultimately, confidence in the religion, or stronger faith, comes from actual proof, i.e. prayers being answered.

It is at the point where actual proof becomes a reality that a member's faith begins to entail some degree of a priori belief. That is to say, on the basis of prior experience, the seasoned Buddhist has some degree of expectation that new challenges will be met and overcome, even though on one level the obstacles may seem insurmountable.

Ultimately, faith is an intangible which fuels the daily actions of practice and study. Practice and study in turn become real-life causes, the effects of which ultimately instill greater faith. In this way, the aspects of faith, practice and study comprise a long-term process by which a believer achieves an endlessly elevating condition of happiness and fulfillment.

The practice of Nichiren Shoshu is made up of two parts—practice for oneself and practice for others. Practice for oneself refers to the daily chanting of Nam-myoho-renge-kyo to the Gohonzon. In addition to this, each Nichiren Shoshu member performs a morning and evening recitation of two chapters of the Lotus Sutra. This recitation combined with the chanting of *daimoku* is known as *gongyo.* The purpose of *gongyo* is to activate the dormant Nam-myoho-renge-kyo within and to instill a sense of discipline, so crucial to the Buddhist process. In addition, *gongyo* creates a rhythmical flow to life which allows each believer to make full use of every moment and every effect created through the power of Nam-myoho-renge-kyo.

The practice for others which Nichiren Daishonin expounded is that of teaching them about the faith of Nichiren Shoshu. Teaching others about Nam-myoho-renge-kyo and the Gohonzon is known in Japanese as *shakubuku.* Rather than being a process of proselytization for the simple purpose of developing or expanding the religious organizational structure, *shakubuku* implies making people aware of the limitations within their own lives and teaching the Buddhist practice as a valid methodology for dealing with difficulties and attaining a greater degree of happiness.

Practice for oneself and for others should not be viewed as two separate things. The Nichiren Shoshu believer practices for others not only for their sake, but for his own as well. Altruism and Buddhist mercy do not come easily to the human being, but Buddhism would claim that they do emerge naturally as a result of effort, because they are fundamental aspects of the Buddha nature within. The Buddhist recognizes that happiness which cannot be shared is rather limited in its scope. Buddhism teaches that the deepest happiness is that which can be shared in human bonding.

Buddhist study is something quite different from the traditional concept. It implies an active, integrated examination of what is happening in daily life and an attempt to tie those happenings into the theories and teachings of Buddhism in order to further develop one's faith and practice. Such an effort and examination can make sense out of real, daily events and place those events into greater perspective. What follows is a section in which the more basic and all-encompassing theories of Buddhism will be discussed. These theories, when put into practice by using tools of the Buddhist teaching we have just finished discussing, eventually can lead human beings to a complete understanding of both the nature and function of life.

REFERENCES

Fundamentals of Buddhism. Y. Kirimura. Los Angeles: World Tribune Press, 1982.

Scripture of the Lotus Blossom of the Fine Dharma. Translated by Leon Hurvitz. New York: Columbia University Press, 1976.

Soka Gakkai International President Daisaku Ikeda confers with Dr. Linus Pauling on issues confronting humankind, one in an ongoing series of such meetings he has hosted with thinkers and dignitaries worldwide.

Professor Norman Cousins is greeted by SGI President Ikeda at the Calabasas, California campus of the Soka University at Los Angeles complex. These conferences offer a means to exchange viewpoints and share the insights of Nichiren Daishonin's Buddhism with others.

Taiseki-ji, the head temple of Nichiren Shoshu in Japan.

The Soka University, Los Angeles campus in the hills above Malibu, California.

NSA General Director George M. Williams gives a seminar on orthodox Buddhism at Tufts University in Boston. Mr. Williams has given scores of such seminars throughout the country in the past two decades.

The NSA World Peace Ikeda Auditorium in Santa Monica, California.

3
Basics of Buddhist Theory

The True Entity of All Phenomena

Theoretical proof, the second of the three criteria for evaluating religious teachings, means that, to be considered valid, a particular doctrine must be logically consistent and not contradict itself. In this chapter we will examine some of the basic aspects of the Buddhist theoretical framework. We have already explained in the preceding section how Nichiren Daishonin used the Lotus Sutra as a scriptural reference to support his teaching of Nammyoho-renge-kyo. Similarly, in giving a theoretical rationale for his teaching, he drew on the philosophical system developed by the Great Teacher T'ien-t'ai on the basis of the Lotus Sutra.

The Lotus Sutra, as already mentioned, teaches that all beings are equally endowed with the Buddha nature and that all are therefore capable of attaining Buddhahood. The sutra conveys this message in several ways. Its first suggestion of a potential for universal enlightenment comes in a passage from the *Hoben* (second) chapter of the Lotus Sutra which refers to "the true entity of all phenomena" (Jap. *shoho jisso*). T'ien-t'ai used this passage as his scriptural authority in establishing his philosophical system.

People of every age have come repeatedly to the realization that phenomena in this world are fleeting and uncertain. This realization has prompted the search for an eternal, unchanging truth. Different teachings offer different explanations of the relationship between this absolute truth and the visible world that we experience. Some hold that the ultimate truth governs this world from a higher realm. Others say that it lies beyond or behind phenomena, or that phenomena are an illusion and the ultimate truth alone is real. According to the Lotus Sutra, the phenomena we perceive in everyday life and the ultimate reality are "two but not two." All things, just as they are, are manifesting the true entity of life.

First, let us look at "all phenomena" and "the true entity" as "two." Phenomena are those aspects of life which can be perceived through the senses or otherwise observed, measured, quantified, explained by reason or grasped with the mind. They are by nature manifold, transient and subject to change. The true entity, on the other hand, is that aspect of life that is one and only one, eternal and unchanging. It is the mystic dimension of life, beyond the reach of reason or the senses. However, these two differing aspects of life are also "not two"; it is impossible that they could ever exist independently. Phenomena are the manifestations of the true entity and so cannot exist without it, while the true entity lies nowhere apart from its phenomenal manifestations.

This concept, though somewhat difficult to grasp, has radical implications. First of all, if the true entity is manifested in all phenomena, then all people are equally endowed with the ultimate truth. All are thus capable of attaining Buddhahood and are inherently worthy of respect. Moreover, enlightenment cannot be confined to a special place, nor can it be the exclusive province of a single person or group of persons. Anyone, just as he is, can become a Buddha.

Three Thousand Worlds in a Single Life-Moment

The concept of "the true entity of all phenomena" was developed and expanded by the Great Teacher T'ien-t'ai into a philosophical system called *ichinen sanzen,* or 3,000 realms in a single moment of life. *Ichinen sanzen* is a world view explaining the mutually inclusive relationship of all phenomena and the ultimate truth. *Ichinen,* or "one mind," is also translated as the life-moment. It is the true entity of life at each moment. *Sanzen,* literally "three thousand," represents the phenomenal world. Of course, there are more than 3,000 phenomena in the universe, as phenomena come in endless variety. The number 3,000 indicates the invariable laws according to which the true entity manifests itself as phenomena. This figure is derived by multiplying the component principles of *ichinen sanzen.* First, take the Ten Worlds or states of life, each of which possesses all ten within itself. Multiplying these makes 100 worlds. Each of these worlds is endowed with ten factors, for a total, when multiplied, of 1,000 factors. Each of these thousand factors operates in three realms, giving a

One 一 ICHI

Mind 念 NEN

Three 三 SAN

Thousand 千 ZEN

total of 3,000 realms. *Ichinen sanzen* is an intricate analysis of the phenomenal world, showing its moment-to-moment interfusion with the ultimate reality.

The Ten Worlds

Now we will examine the component principles of the *ichinen sanzen* system. Let us begin with what are called the Ten Worlds (*jikkai*). These are ten states or conditions of existence. One might be tempted to think of them as states of mind, but this would not be entirely accurate. Rather, they are states of life itself that one experiences with his subjective being and that are manifested in both the spiritual and physical aspects of his life. According to the *ichinen sanzen* theory, everyone possesses the potential for all ten, and can shift from one to another at any moment, according to the nature of his interaction with the environment. That is, at each moment, one of the Ten Worlds is being manifested and the other nine are dormant. From the lowest to highest, they are:

(1) Hell (*jigoku*): This is a state of suffering and despair, in which one has almost no freedom of action. It is characterized by the impulse to destroy oneself and everything around one.

(2) Hunger (*gaki*): Hunger is the state of being controlled by insatiable desire for money, power, status, or whatever. While desires are inherent in life in any of the Ten Worlds, in this state one is totally at the mercy of his cravings and cannot control them.

(3) Animality (*chikusho*): One in this state is ruled by instinct and exhibits neither reason nor moral sense nor ability to make long-range judgments. He operates by the law of the jungle, so to speak. He will not hesitate to take advantage of those weaker than himself and fawns on those who are stronger.

(4) Anger (*shura*): The states of Hell, Hunger and Animality are collectively called the three evil paths. Life in these conditions is dominated by instinctive desires and passions. In this next state,

Anger, awareness of ego emerges, but it is a ravening, distorted ego, determined to best others at all cost and seeing everything as a potential threat to itself. In this state one values only himself and holds others in contempt. He is strongly attached to the idea of his own superiority and cannot bear to admit that anyone excels him in anything. The three evil paths plus Anger are called the four lower worlds.

(5) Humanity (*nin*), sometimes called Tranquillity: In this state one controls his passions and desires with reason, enabling the more appropriately human qualities such as love and benevolence to emerge. A person in this state can exercise sound judgment, distinguish right from wrong and generally behave in a humane fashion.

(6) Heaven (*ten*), also called Rapture: This is a state of intense joy or rapture stemming, for example, from the fulfillment of some desire, a sense of physical well-being, or spiritual content-ment. Though intense, the joy experienced in this state is short-lived and extremely vulnerable to external influences.

The six states from Hell to Heaven are called the six paths or six lower worlds. They have in common the fact that their emergence or disappearance is governed solely by external circumstances. Take the example of a person obsessed by the desire to find some-one to love him (Hunger). When he at last does meet that person, he feels ecstatic and fulfilled (Heaven). By and by potential rivals appear on the scene and he is seized by jealousy (Anger). Eventual-ly his possessiveness drives his loved one away. Crushed by despair (Hell), he feels life is no longer worth living. In this way, a majority of people spends most of the time being shuttled back and forth among these six states without ever realizing that they are being controlled by their reactions to the environment. Any happiness or satisfaction to be gained in these states depends totally upon cir-cumstances and is therefore transient and subject to change. While in the six worlds, however, one does not see this but bases his entire happiness, indeed the whole of his identity, on externals.

The next two states, Learning and Realization, come about when one recognizes that everything experienced in the six paths is impermanent and begins to seek some lasting truth. These two states plus the next two, Bodhisattva and Buddhahood, are together called the four noble worlds. Unlike the six paths, which are in essence passive reactions to the environment, these four higher states are achieved only through deliberate effort.

(7) Learning (*shomon*): In this state, one seeks the truth through the teachings or experience of others. The Japanese word *shomon* (Skt. *shravaka*) literally means "voice-hearer" and originally indicated the Buddha's disciples who had personally heard him expound his teachings.

(8) Realization (*engaku*): This state is very similar to Learning, except that one seeks the truth not through others' teachings but through his own direct perception of the world. *Engaku* (Skt. *pratyekka-buddha*) originally meant one who independently arrived at an understanding of Buddhist truths.

Learning and Realization are together called the two vehicles. Having realized the mutability of things, people in these states have won a measure of independence and are no longer prisoner to their own reactions as one is in the six paths. However, they often tend to be contemptuous of people in the six paths who have not yet reached this understanding. In addition, their search for truth is primarily self-oriented, so there is a potential for egotism in these two states.

(9) Bodhisattva (*bosatsu*): A bodhisattva is one who aspires to achieve supreme enlightenment, but who is equally determined to enable all other beings to do the same. Conscious of the bonds that link him to all others, he realizes that any happiness he alone enjoys is illusory and incomplete, and he devotes himself to alleviating others' suffering even at the risk of his life. Those in this state find their greatest satisfaction in altruistic behavior.

The states from Hell to Bodhisattva are collectively termed the nine worlds. This expression is often used in contrast to the tenth world, Buddhahood, to indicate unenlightened states of life.

(10) Buddhahood (*butsu* or *hotoke*): Buddhahood is a state beyond the ability of words to express. With that remark as a premise, we can venture to partially describe it as a state of perfect freedom, in which one is enlightened to the ultimate truth of life. It is characterized by infinite compassion and boundless wisdom. In this state, one can harmoniously resolve what appear from the standpoint of the nine worlds to be insoluble contradictions. The Nirvana Sutra describes the attributes of the Buddha's life as a perfected true self, perfect freedom throughout eternity, a life purified of illusion and absolute happiness.

The Mutual Possession of the Ten Worlds

The Ten Worlds were originally thought of as distinct physical realms into which beings were born as a result of accumulated karma. For example, human beings were born in the world of Humanity, animals in the world of Animality and gods in the world of Heaven. Beings in Hell were thought to be imprisoned below the earth, and beings in Hunger were depicted as hungry ghosts with huge, distended bellies and needle-thin throats, incapable of assuaging their terrible hunger. According to this idea, one could shift from one world to another only at the juncture between death and rebirth. In the Lotus Sutra, however, one can glimpse a more sophisticated view of the Ten Worlds. The *ichinen sanzen* theory asserts that there are no realms of reality divorced from the one that we experience: no hell underground, no heaven in the sky, and no paradisiacal Buddha lands in remote corners of the universe. (This does not rule out the possibility of life on other planets, which is perfectly consistent with Buddhist thought.) The Ten Worlds are instead viewed as conditions of life which all people have the potential to experience. At any moment, one of the ten will be manifest and the other nine dormant, but there is always the potential for change.

This principle is expressed as the mutual possession of the Ten Worlds (*jikkai gogu*). This principle states that each of the Ten Worlds possesses all ten within itself. For example, a person who is at this moment in the state of Hell may at the next moment either remain in Hell or manifest any of the other nine states. The most important implication of this principle is that all people in whatever state of life have the ever-present potential to manifest Buddhahood.

In the course of a day we experience different states from moment to moment in response to our interaction with the environment. The sight of another's suffering will call forth the compassionate world of Bodhisattva, and the loss of a loved one will plunge us into Hell. However, each person has one or more worlds around which his life-activities center and to which he tends to revert when external stimuli subside. This world or worlds is called the basic life-tendency and has been established by that individual through his prior actions. Some people's lives revolve around the three evil paths, some move back and forth among the six lower worlds, and some are primarily motivated by the desire to seek the truth which characterizes the two vehicles. The purpose of Buddhist practice is to elevate the basic life-tendency and eventually establish Buddhahood as one's fundamental state.

Establishing Buddhahood as our basic life-tendency does not mean that we rid ourselves of the other nine worlds. All these states are integral and necessary aspects of life. Without the sufferings of Hell, we could never feel compassion for others. Without the instinctive desires represented by Hunger and Animality, we would forget to eat, sleep and reproduce ourselves, and soon become extinct. Even someone who has established Buddhahood as his fundamental life-tendency will still continue to experience the joys and sorrows of the nine worlds. However, they will not control him, and he will not define himself in terms of them. Based on the life-tendency of Buddhahood, his nine worlds will be harmonized and function to benefit both himself and those around him.

The Ten Factors

The Ten Worlds are a classification of the different states manifested by a living being within the flow of time. Each of the Ten Worlds has its own unique characteristics—Hell, for example, being very different from Learning. The ten factors (*junyoze*), on the other hand, is an analysis of the pattern of existence common to life in any of the Ten Worlds. Life in Hell, Hunger, Animality or any of the other Ten Worlds possesses the same ten factors. The word *nyoze*, literally "like this," prefixed to the names of the ten factors in Japanese, indicates that all, just as they are, manifest the true entity of life. The ten factors also enables us to understand how life shifts from one of the Ten Worlds to another. They are:

(1) Appearance (*nyoze-so*): Those aspects of things which can be perceived or discerned from the outside. Appearance includes such attributes as color, form and behavior, and in terms of human beings points to the physical side of our existence, including the body and its functions.

(2) Nature (*nyoze-sho*): Internal disposition or those qualities which cannot be discerned from the outside. In terms of human life, nature indicates the spiritual aspects of life such as mind and consciousness.

(3) Entity (*nyoze-tai*): The entity or essence of life which manifests itself as external appearance and inner nature but is itself neither. It is the entity of life in any of the Ten Worlds.

These first three factors describe life from a static viewpoint. They analyze what life *is*. The next six factors describe the dynamic functions of life. Power and influence describe life's workings in terms of space, while internal cause, relation, latent effect and manifest effect all deal with causality and explain life's functions in terms of time.

(4) Power (*nyoze-riki*): Life's inherent capacity to act, its potential strength or energy to achieve something. Each of the Ten Worlds has its corresponding power. For example, life in the state of Humanity has the power to uphold ethical standards, and life in the state of Bodhisattva has the power to alleviate others' suffering.

(5) Influence (*nyoze-sa*): The action or movement produced when life's latent power is activated. It is the exertion of influence, whether good or evil, in thought, speech or action.

These two factors of power and influence presuppose the existence of some external object toward which movement or action is directed. Entity, when accompanied by the dynamic factors of power and influence, may be thought of as an autonomous "self" that can act in relation to other existences. The next four factors explain how the actions of that "self" cause it to shift from one of the Ten Worlds to another.

(6) Internal cause (*nyoze-in*): The cause latent in life, which simultaneously contains a potential effect. A good cause produces a good effect, and a bad cause, a bad effect.

(7) Relation (*nyoze-en*): The auxiliary cause or environmental stimulus which helps karma (internal cause) to produce its effect. Though also called external cause, it is not the environment itself but the connection between life and the environment. When activated by relation, an internal cause undergoes a change and simultaneously produces a new latent effect. It is also through the function of relation that latent effects become manifest.

(8) Latent effect (*nyoze-ka*): The potential effect produced in the depths of life when the internal cause is activated by relation. Since both internal cause and latent effect are dormant in the depths of life, there is no time gap between the two such as that which often occurs between an action and its perceivable result.

(9) Manifest effect (*nyoze-ho*): The concrete, perceptible result which emerges after the passing of time as a consequence of internal cause and latent effect.

A brief example may help to clarify the six factors from power through manifest effect. Imagine a fledgling sculptor. His capacity for artistic dedication (power) finds expression in actual efforts (influence) to perfect the use of hammer and chisel. Through his interaction with wood or stone (relation), his innate artistic ability (internal cause) is stimulated (latent effect), and in time he will become a master artist (manifest effect).

(10) Consistency from beginning to end (*nyoze-hommatsu-kukyo-*

to): The integrating factor that unifies all the other nine factors at each moment in a single entity of life. Where there is one factor, all the other nine will invariably be present. Moreover, if one defines the first three factors as entity (beginning) and the next six as function (end), then both beginning and end, that is, the entity and function of all phenomena, are inseparable.

The Three Realms

The three realms (*san seken*) are the last of the component principles of *ichinen sanzen*. They are the realm of the five components (*go'on seken*), the realm of living beings (*shujo seken*) and the realm of the environment (*kokudo seken*). Living beings are individual entities which manifest one or another of the Ten Worlds. The five components are the constituents that, in traditional Buddhist thought, combine to form a living being. The environment is where living beings carry out their activities. We can think of the three realms as the three dimensions of the phenomenal world in which the Ten Worlds manifest themselves.

First, the five components are:

(1) Form (*shiki*): The physical aspect of life which possesses such attributes as shape and color. Form also indicates the five sensory organs—eyes, ears, nose, mouth and skin—through which one perceives the outer world.

(2) Perception (*ju*): The function of receiving external information through the six sensory organs (the five sensory organs plus "mind," which integrates sensory impressions).

(3) Conception (*so*): The function by which one forms an idea or conception about what has been perceived.

(4) Volition (*gyo*): The will to take some action toward what has been perceived. (Action itself would be classified as "form.")

(5) Consciousness (*shiki*): The discerning function of life which can make value judgments, distinguish good from evil, and so forth. Consciousness also functions to support and integrate the other four components.

When the five components are classified according to the material and spiritual aspects of life, form corresponds to the physical aspect and the other four to the spiritual aspect. However, since Buddhism holds that the material and spiritual aspects of life are inseparable, there is no form without perception, conception, volition and consciousness, nor can there be consciousness without form, perception, conception and volition. The five components must be understood as a whole and grasped in terms of their interaction.

The differences of the Ten Worlds are reflected in the workings of the five components. For example, in the state of Hell one will perceive and react to a given phenomenon quite differently than he would in the state of Bodhisattva. The karma he creates thereby will also differ. In this way, the five components are colored by the individual karma formed in successive lifetimes, and they also work to accumulate further karma. The word *on* of *go'on*, translated as component, originally had two meanings: to accumulate and to veil or obscure. In their unenlightened states, the five components work to "accumulate" suffering and "obscure" the truth within. In Buddhahood, they work to "accumulate" good fortune and are "veiled" in compassion.

Next, we have the realm of living beings. What Buddhism terms "living beings" are defined as beings who are sentient. For our purposes we can think of them as human beings. According to Buddhist thought, all living beings, from those in Hell to those in the state of Buddhahood, are formed by a temporary union of the five components—temporary because it will disintegrate at death. Whichever one of the Ten Worlds underlies the workings of the five components will also be manifested in the living being formed by those five components.

Since living beings are viewed as a temporary union of the five components, the question arises why a separate realm should be established for them apart from the realm of the five components. The answer is that these two realms view the living being from different angles. The realm of the five components analyzes the living being into component physical and spiritual workings, while the realm of the living being views him as an integrated individual capable of interaction with the environment. The realm of living beings can also be interpreted in the plural to mean a group of living beings.

In this sense, the realm of living beings indicates the truth that we live in a state of perpetual interrelation and mutual dependence with other living beings. However, we often fall under the illusion that our "self" is somehow absolute and independent of all others. Buddhism teaches that all suffering ultimately stems from this egocentricity. The idea that "living beings are no more than a temporary union of the five components" was intended to help break this attachment to the concept of oneself as fixed and absolute.

Lastly, we have the realm of the environment. The realm of the environment is the place where living beings dwell and upon which they depend for survival. It includes insentient life forms such as grass, trees, mountains, rivers, and so on. Whichever of the Ten Worlds a living being manifests will also be manifested in his environment.

As we have said, the Ten Worlds were originally conceived of as distinct physical environments. Hell was thought to be below the ground, Heaven atop the mythical Mt. Sumeru, and so forth. According to the *ichinen sanzen* theory, however, the land itself, like living beings, possesses all Ten Worlds. The only difference is that the environment has no independent life-condition; it manifests one or another of the Ten Worlds in response to the life-condition of the living beings inhabiting it. For example, a person in Hunger will experience a given environment in a different way than he would in the state of Humanity. The most significant implication here is that the human being can transform his environment by elevating his own state of life. There is no special place where one must go to attain enlightenment, and no special realm where the Buddha dwells. Rather, by bringing forth his innate Buddhahood, any individual can make his surroundings the Buddha land.

While the Ten Worlds and ten factors are common to all beings, the three realms explain that no two beings are alike. The most basic differences expressed in the three realms are those of the Ten Worlds, as we have seen. However, we find still further, individual differences. For example, even among living beings in the same world of Learning, no two will have exactly the same physical form, and no two will perceive, conceive and respond to the world in exactly the same way. Moreover, no two will have exactly the same environment.

There are a number of concepts that, while not included among the component principles of *ichinen sanzen*, nevertheless derive from the *ichinen sanzen* theory and are implicit in it. Here we would like to look briefly at two of the most important ones.

The Oneness of Body and Mind

The principle of the oneness of body and mind (*shiki shin funi*) describes the inseparable relationship of life's physical and spiritual aspects. Matter and spirit are two categories into which all phenomena may be classified. The word *funi* of *shiki shin funi* is an abbreviation of both *nini funi* ("two but not two") and *funi nini* ("not two but two"). These rather paradoxical expressions mean that matter and spirit may be seen as separate from the viewpoint of phenomena but are one and inseparable from the viewpoint of the true entity. We can perhaps see this principle most clearly in the first three of the ten factors, which, as we said, describe the reality of life. External appearance (the physical) and inner nature (the spiritual) are the phenomenal aspects of life. The entity manifests both appearance and nature but is itself neither. Though appearance and nature have different qualities, they are unified at the essential level by the fact that they share the same entity.

Contemporary research in the fields of medicine, physiology and psychology has confirmed the reciprocal influence of body and mind. However, the Buddhist concept of the oneness of body and mind goes beyond this psychosomatic relationship, grasping the ultimate reality which makes that relationship possible in the first place. It defines life not in terms of its material or spiritual aspects but in terms of the entity which finds its expression in these two aspects.

Buddhism thus rejects any essential dichotomy of body and

mind. Nor does it postulate one as the basis of the other. For the Buddhist there is no such thing as pure matter or pure spirit. There is only life itself, and wherever there is life it invariably manifests both a material and a spiritual aspect. To give an illustration, a nickel invariably has both a head and a tail. Head and tail can be viewed as different sides of the coin, but they can never be fundamentally separated, as both are integral aspects of the nickel. Not only sentient beings such as humans and animals but insentient life forms as well possess both physical and spiritual aspects.

This principle can also serve as an approach to the Buddhist view of death. Since matter and spirit can never exist independently, Buddhism categorically denies the existence of a soul which leaves the body at death and is later reborn into a new body. Rather, the true entity of life forever repeats two alternating phases: the manifest (life) and the latent (death). While in the manifest phase, life exhibits both physical and spiritual functions; in the latent phase, these functions become dormant. When triggered by an appropriate external cause (conception), life emerges from the dormant phase and reappears in the world, manifesting both a material and a spiritual aspect.

Since the Ten Worlds are manifested in both aspects of life, Buddhahood is not a purely spiritual experience. The chanting of Nam-myoho-renge-kyo is a practice involving both body and mind, and its effects likewise appear in both the physical and spiritual sides of a believer's life.

The Oneness of Life and Its Environment

The principle of the oneness of life and its environment (*esho funi*) describes the inseparable relationship of the individual and his environment. One generally has a tendency to regard the environment as something separate from oneself, and from the viewpoint of observable phenomena, we are justified in drawing this distinction. However, from the viewpoint of life's entity, the individual and his environment are one and inseparable. *Funi* of *esho funi* means the same thing that it does in the oneness of body and mind or *shiki shin funi*: "two but not two" and "not two but two." The true entity of life invariably manifests itself in both a living subject and an objective environment. These two aspects form yet another classification of "all phenomena."

Of the three realms, the realm of the five components and the realm of living beings are traditionally viewed as "life" in "the oneness of life and its environment." However, if the realm of living beings is interpreted in the plural, it may also be viewed as "environment." "Life" indicates a subjective "self" which experiences the karmic effects of past actions. The environment is the objective realm where the karmic effects which that life experiences take shape. Environment here does not mean one overall context in which all beings live. Each living being has his own unique environment in which the effects of his individual karma appear. The word *esho* of *esho funi* is a contraction of *eho* (the objective environment) and *shoho* (the living self or subject). The word *ho* in both these terms is the same *ho* as in *nyoze-ho*, or manifest effect. The effects of one's karma, both good and bad, manifest themselves both in one's self and in the environment, because these are two integral phases of the same entity.

The results of biological and ecological research have demonstrated the subtle interaction of living beings and their environments. However, this is still interaction at the phenomenal level where life and its environment are distinct. The principle of the oneness of life and its environment describes the true entity which manifests these two aspects and makes their interaction possible.

Since both life and its environment share the same entity, whichever one of the Ten Worlds an individual manifests will be mirrored in his environment. This idea has important implications. First, as already mentioned, one need not seek enlightenment in a particular place. Wherever he is, under whatever circumstances, he can bring forth his innate Buddhahood, thus transforming his experience of the environment. This is an act of freedom whereby the individual in effect liberates himself from control by circumstances. For example, if he sufficiently elevates his life, he will not be crushed by adversity but can command the

strength and wisdom to use it constructively for his own development. Moreover, as he accumulates good karma through Buddhist practice, the effects of the karma will become apparent not
only in himself but also in his environment, in the form of im-
proved material circumstances, greater respect from others, and
so forth. From the standpoint of *ichinen sanzen*, one's environment stretches out to encompass the whole dimension of space.
One person's enlightenment is therefore not confined to himself
but exerts an influence on his family, community, nation, and
ultimately all humanity. The principle of the oneness of life and its
environment is the rationale for asserting that the Buddhist practice of individuals can in time work a transformation in society, establishing a "Buddha land" here in this world.

Theoretical and Actual Ichinen Sanzen

So far, we have outlined the structure of the theory of *ichinen
sanzen* and seen that in essence it is a philosophical system describ-
ing the perfect interfusion of the true entity of life and the
phenomenal world. In the light of *ichinen sanzen,* any person is a
potential Buddha, and wherever one is, he or she can establish the
Buddha land.

This, however, is talking about potential, not the reality that
most people experience. To indicate this gap between potential
and actuality, T'ien-t'ai expounded two views of *ichinen sanzen*—
theoretical and actual. Theoretical *ichinen sanzen* (*ri no ichinen
sanzen*) is the life of common mortals, or unenlightened beings. It
is called theoretical because the potential for Buddhahood is not
manifest but is present only in theory. Actual *ichinen sanzen* (*ji no
ichinen sanzen*) is the life of the Buddha, in which the state of Buddhahood is fully manifest, playing out through the workings of his
own life and his interaction with others. The practical problem is:
How can common mortals bring out and enjoy their latent
Buddhahood?

As was previously explained, the Gohonzon manifests the life
of Nichiren Daishonin, a Buddha fully enlightened to the Law.
The Gohonzon is thus the embodiment of actual *ichinen sanzen*, or

reality fully manifesting the state of Buddhahood. By chanting Nam-myoho-renge-kyo to the Gohonzon we fuse our lives with it, and in consequence our own Buddha nature begins to emerge. This is something actually experienced by those who undertake the practice of Nichiren Daishonin's teaching. That experience is known as actual proof—the perceivable effects brought about by the emergence of one's Buddha nature—and is the subject of the next section.

REFERENCES

Buddhism: The Living Philosophy. Daisaku Ikeda. Tokyo: The East Publications, Inc., 1977.

Choose Life. Arnold Toynbee and Daisaku Ikeda. London: Oxford University Press, 1976.

Dialogue on Life, vol. 1. Daisaku Ikeda, Yoichi Kawada and Masahiro Kitagawa. Tokyo: Nichiren Shoshu International Center, 1976.

4
Living as a Buddhist

The Quest for Enlightenment

Having thus far focused upon the prescribed practice and theoretical explanations that form the basis of Nichiren Shoshu Buddhism, we now turn our attention to the third and most important criterion by which to judge a religion—that of actual proof. It is this standard that concerns itself with the real-life application and results of religious practice and theory.

Ultimately, the result of the Buddhist faith for each person who practices it is said to be enlightenment. Now, enlightenment is a concept which has been expounded upon and argued about for as long as mankind has been cognizant of how much it did not know. The enlightenment of Nichiren Shoshu is so profound that it defies verbal description. Nevertheless, it could be said to encompass a number of dimensions.

On one level, enlightenment might be defined as a life-condition of absolute happiness and confidence about life. On this level, not only are all of life's ramifications at the present moment completely understood, but as a result of such total awareness, causes can be made to insure a joyous and secure future.

Because Buddhism speaks of the oneness of mind and body as well as the inseparability of the person and the environment, the Buddhist definition of enlightenment must also take these concepts into account. In other words, the enlightenment of Nichiren Shoshu is in no way limited to the spiritual realm. A person's enlightenment is not only reflected in his or her emotional confidence level or profound wisdom about the universe and life. That enlightenment must, by definition, also be evident in such areas as material fortune and physical health.

Perhaps even more important, the enlightenment of the Nichiren Shoshu believer is something that reaches far beyond the limited realm of his or her immediate environment. The greatest impact of Buddhist enlightenment is that it is employed to actually enlighten others. From the standpoint of the Mahayana Buddhist tradition—expounded by all Buddhas, from Shakyamuni to Nichiren Daishonin—the ultimate goal of the Buddhist religion is the shared enlightenment of all humanity. This shared enlightenment, it is believed, will eventually manifest itself in a world of human beings at peace with themselves and living in harmony with nature.

Obviously, enlightenment, when expressed in such terms as the preceding, is a goal which seems both lofty and distant. Nevertheless, it is a real-life goal and, as such, is distinctly different from the afterlife or spiritually intangible objectives often expressed as the greatest promises of more traditional Western religions. Also, in the actual daily practice of Buddhism, much more emphasis is placed on the *process* of living than its end result. The Buddhist approach is entirely common sense. In fact, it is in the occurrence of significant daily events that the actual proof of the Buddhist faith shines for the practitioner.

Pursuit of Desires

The process of living as a Buddhist has come to be known as human revolution. This human revolution is considered by Buddhists to be the fundamental revolution—the change of life which must occur as a catalyst to all other change, be it social, political, environmental or whatever. Human revolution entails both the elevation of one's basic life-condition and the undertaking of positive action as a prerequisite to any external change.

The process of human revolution is, of course, based on faith in the Buddhist practice and its course is defined by one's own needs and desires. This latter aspect is a most unique feature of the Nichiren Shoshu faith. In many Western religions which focus on the existence of a transcendent God, one is encouraged to live life in accordance with the desires of God rather than being swayed by more personal, implicitly selfish motivations. God-fearing people often end up doing more what they think they should do than what they want to do.

Similarly, earlier Buddhist teachings, known as the Theravada school, also urged the suppression of personal desires for the accomplishment of a holy purpose. The rationale behind this was that our senses tend to delude us with regard to the world around us. Since our senses are functions of our body, early Buddhism proposed that suppression of earthly desires—desires associated with bodily needs such as hunger, shelter, sex, and so on—would negate the detrimental aspects of physical existence and allow the human being to manifest his or her full spiritual potential.

Nichiren Daishonin's Buddhism, however, is a religion which teaches the oneness of mind and body. The idea of suppressing one's earthly, physical desires for the attainment of some greater spiritual good is obviously contradictory to such an idea. True Buddhism does ask that the human being come to recognize the eternal aspect of his or her own life while perceiving the essential transience of all phenomena. Nevertheless, this awareness is something to be achieved on both a spiritual and a material plane.

Therefore, rather than demanding the suppression of desires as a prerequisite to attaining enlightenment, Nichiren Shoshu suggests that the very pursuit of those desires is what elevates one's life-condition to an enlightened level. The fact that true Buddhism proposes that desires literally transform into enlightenment (*bonno soku bodai*) is what makes this religion accessible to every human being and provides the motivation to do human revolution. After all, each of us truly wants to pursue our desires.

Some might argue that a religion which proposes that man give free rein to his desires is being rather irresponsible. After all, have not experience and history shown us time and time again that man's own ego tends to sow the seeds for his own destruction and create untold suffering for the generations which follow? It is in response to this concern that Buddhism holds fast to its essential premise—the inviolable dignity and Buddha nature of each and every single human being.

The problem, Buddhism postulates, lies not in the essential nature of the human being but rather in the inability of the human to tap that nature. To this end, Nichiren Daishonin clarified Nammyoho-renge-kyo as the core of human life and advocated chanting as the key to unlocking that core.

Earthly Desires 煩 BON

悩 NO

Essentially Equal 即 SOKU

菩 BO

Enlightenment 提 DAI

Buddhism submits that the tendency of the human being to give in to his or her baser tendencies and thus create disastrous future effects is not a function of some inherent human flaw. There is no original sin in Buddhism. Rather, human beings over the ages have become deluded with regard to the true nature of their own lives. They vest their fortune in some transcendent or vague concept of God or fate and thereby abdicate responsibility for their lives to someone or something else. Or they deny the existence of a greater reality altogether and think that simply living for the present, drawing the greatest sustenance they can from their immediate phenomenal reality, is what life is all about. In either case, the Daishonin would claim that human beings tend to delude themselves about the true nature of things and operate from a level of fundamental darkness or error (*gampon-no mumyo*).

In his writings, Nichiren Daishonin asks that we recognize the irrevocable reality that "the body is the palace of the ninth consciousness, the unchanging reality which reigns over all life's functions." What he is referring to is the unconscious reality of the Buddha nature that eternally exists within—the ultimate teaching of the Lotus Sutra that Nichiren Daishonin crystallized as Nammyoho-renge-kyo.

Without going into a detailed explanation of the "nine consciousnesses" expounded in Buddhist theory, suffice it to say that the ninth consciousness is held to be the eternal, unchangeable essence in each of our lives. The eighth consciousness, on the other hand, is known as the "karma storehouse" wherein all the causes and effects of one's life are stored. This is similar to the psychological school of thought which teaches that nothing is ever forgotten or discarded from one's life. In any event, we are talking here about things which totally exist in the subconscious levels of human existence. The first seven consciousnesses deal with aspects of the conscious mind, such as the five senses, thinking, judgment, and so on. Buddhism, like psychology, explains that man's conscious thought and mind are simply the tip of a far deeper iceberg.

The point here is that man's incorrect tendencies and ideas stem from the eighth consciousness. They have been ingrained there by previous negative causes and teachings. The fundamental darkness of man's life, therefore, rather than existing at the core of his being, is simply a dark or unenlightened area existing at very deep levels of his unconscious life. Chanting Nam-myoho-renge-kyo activates the "fundamental enlightenment" (*gampon-no hossho*) of the ninth consciousness, thereby illuminating that which was previously dark within the karma storehouse. The effect is similar to turning on the light in a dark attic. What was previously black and frightening is now illuminated and available for constructive use. Through the Buddhist practice, that within our lives which previously served to hurt us is transformed and becomes a force for the creation of value.

Developing the Highest Ego

It is on the basis of all of this that Buddhism teaches us to pursue our desires. Even if those desires emanate from a basically nega-tive aspect of our being, the practice of Buddhism will illuminate that aspect and the law of cause and effect will clearly show what changes need to be made. The wisdom and effort to make those changes are the key elements of the human revolution—elements found within rather than provided from without.

Ultimately, the process of human revolution leads to the devel-opment of what Buddhism terms the "higher ego"—to be distin-guished from the lower ego which has historically created so much of a problem for mankind. In a lecture given in 1974 at UCLA, Soka Gakkai International President Daisaku Ikeda expanded on this notion of the higher ego by saying:

We cannot say that it is stupid to be charmed by fleeting pleasures, or swayed by worldly desires. No. As long as life continues, it is instinctual to want to live, to cherish love and to seek profit.

A life dominated by desire or swayed by external influences is only a superficial expression of the human ego. Enlightenment or awareness of the universal truth underlying all phenomena brings out the most noble and rewarding ego.

This highest ego is the fundamental principle of the universe. It is also the same law which controls the expression of the self within each individual. . . .

Pursuing this true ego does not imply giving up a lesser or more superficial one. The fact is that the highest ego gives new direction to the lesser one.

Civilization advances because of the instincts and desires of men. The pursuit of wealth enables economic growth. The will to defy the winter cold led to the development of natural science. Somehow, love, which is a desire, inspired literature.

Some schools of Buddhism teach the suppression of all earthly desire. Because they equate desires with the mortal flesh, they even condone self-immolation. However, desires arise from the innermost core of life. They are absolutely indestructible. They are the motivating force behind all behavior.

So, it is absolutely necessary to give direction to the superficial ego. This ego is only meaningful when based on the loftier ego. True Buddhism has clarified this highest ego as true human nature. I feel very strongly that our civilization will be able to make meaningful progress only if we understand this point.

As mentioned before, a Buddhist pursuing his or her desires and undergoing the process of human revolution in the quest for enlightenment keeps in mind not only personal fulfillment but also cherishes the hope for a shared enlightenment among all mankind. To this end, the higher ego requires that causes be made in the transpersonal as well as the individual realm. For the Nichiren Shoshu Buddhist, the greatest cause that can be made in order to share the enlightenment of Nam-myoho-renge-kyo is the giving of that teaching to another human being. *Shakubuku*, proselytizing in Nichiren Shoshu Buddhism, is more than just an attempt at enlarging the religious organization. The hope that each person can learn to tap the universal law that lies within, thereby initiating the human revolution on a worldwide level, provides the deepest rationale for *shakubuku*. Buddhists believe that only in the accomplishment of global human revolution can the salvation of all humankind be guaranteed.

Daisaku Ikeda has said that "a great revolution of character in just a single person will help achieve a change in the destiny of a nation and, further, will enable a change in the destiny of all mankind." Although this statement may seem idealistic, almost to the extent of being naive in this day and age, it is still no less valid in the eyes of the Buddhist teaching. From more and more arenas of the human experience, evidence is accumulating which supports the concept of human revolution and points to it as perhaps the only factor which can pull civilization back from the brink of the abyss which it seems to be approaching.

Inflation, energy crises, ineffectual leadership and a host of other problems create an environment of chaos, presenting problems which often seem insoluble. Add to this the ever-present Damocles sword of nuclear warfare and it is difficult to know where to begin to make the challenge. Because these problems affect us on such an insidious psychological level—as opposed to the overt physical threat of actual war or even street crime—the human being tends to move his or her consciousness in the direction of solving these problems through the imagination of new structures, economics, politics, and so on.

This is the real threat—that our attention to changing environmental forms will rob us of the energy and creativity we need to change ourselves. This is not to say that efforts to change the environment are fruitless; rather, human beings must get their priorities straight and recognize that it is the development of their life-condition rather than their mentality that will ultimately solve the problem.

Toward Global Harmony

As the ultimate proof of its validity, Buddhism holds out the dream of a world at peace resulting from the individual human revolution of millions and millions of human beings around the globe. This dream is more than an ideal—it is a stated destination of the entire Buddhist movement. For the individual, the actuality of the Buddhist faith is manifest in the process we refer to as human revolution. For civilization as a whole, the ideals of the Buddhist religion are reflected in an actual social movement known as *kosen-rufu*.

Kosen means to teach the Buddhist religion to all people, and *rufu* means that Buddhism is both well-known and sincerely practiced by people in society. Thus *kosen* indicates the propagation of

Buddhism, and *rufu* the condition which results from this propagation.

From the preceding definition of *kosen-rufu*, it might easily and mistakenly be assumed that *kosen-rufu* is a numerical goal, some pre-set percentage which, when reached, will assure a world at peace. However, *kosen-rufu*, as most other things in the Buddhist scheme of things, is essentially a process. Daisaku Ikeda described it as follows:

Kosen-rufu in no way means a goal. In the fundamental Buddhist sense of the word it is not accurate to regard *kosen-rufu* as something like a fixed terminus. The Daishonin's Buddhism is a teaching of the True Cause, which means that true Buddhism is always moving toward the future. The Daishonin asserted therefore, that (his own) Kamakura era, also, was a time for *kosen-rufu*.

In addition, the Daishonin was indicating an eternal unceasing current of *kosen-rufu* when he said that Nam-myoho-renge-kyo will spread "for 10,000 years and more, throughout all eternity." *Kosen-rufu* is not the terminus of a current, but the current itself, the pulsation in society of living Buddhism.

In short, religion constitutes the foundation of a culture, the soil on which humanity flourishes. When a sound religion is lost, culture decays, creating a great void inside humanity itself. . . . The loss of a sound religion is the very root of the evil which is gnawing at the vitals of modern civilization and culture. At this time of crisis, is it not our mission to build a new culture and revive society?

There are a number of examples in history which demonstrate the nourishment that an appropriate religious awakening gave to a people's culture. In the ancient Indian country of Sravasti, a form of *kosen-rufu* was said to have been attained when one-third of the population practiced Buddhism, another third sympathized with it and the remainder were indifferent or opposed to it. All the people in the country were said to have enjoyed the happiness and prosperity of the culture.

In the first 500 years after the death of Shakyamuni, Ashoka the Great, who had unified all of India through military conquest, gave up war for pacifism. This was due to his conversion to Buddhism. Ashoka went on to establish the first public hospitals and parks, and dedicated his government's efforts to the welfare of the people. He provided the opportunity for many to learn about

Buddhism and promoted its practice while maintaining religious freedom. During this period the culture of India reached a high level.

In the second millenium after Shakyamuni's death, Chinese culture experienced an unprecedented prosperity after T'ien-t'ai converted the emperor as well as the ten most influential sects and had spread the teachings of the Lotus Sutra throughout the country. The Heian culture of Japan (794-1185 A.D.), which has known no equivalent in that country's history, corresponds to the widespread introduction of T'ien-t'ai's Buddhism by the great teacher Dengyo.

Now, in an era almost 3,000 years after Shakyamuni, Nichiren Shoshu members are working diligently for the construction of an eternal, global state of *kosen-rufu* based on the true Buddhism of Nichiren Daishonin. In the Buddhist's mind, this is not some paradisiacal, utopian condition. Rather, *kosen-rufu* might be better described as an entopia—an ever more harmonious, evolving condition of global humanity. It is only natural that human minds will constantly move, and new generations will replace old. Conflict, turmoil and change are a permanent part of the human reality.

Kosen-rufu is not meant to imply an idyllic world in which there is no suffering or pain. Rather, Buddhists aim toward a world in which humans, rather than inflicting pain on one another, unite to face the common challenges that cause mankind to suffer as a whole. Rather than simply making laws to govern themselves, human beings should ideally be able to find the universal law within which will allow them not only to live in peace with one another, but also in peace with the planet from which they draw sustenance.

In his *Gosho,* Nichiren Daishonin says, "Regard suffering and joy as facts of life and continue to chant Nam-myoho-renge-kyo no matter what happens." Ours will never be a world in which suffering completely vanishes; what Buddhism would have happen at the stage of *kosen-rufu* is that humanity share common suffering in the natural process of self-development, rather than inflict suffering upon itself in a headlong rush to self-destruction.

SGI President Ikeda once defined *kosen-rufu* as something like a second Renaissance. He said:

> The ideal of the future must originate from religious faith deep in the human heart. The time has come to take first priority away from external authority and give it to the revolution that must take place in the heart of each human being. This must be the age of the second Renaissance. The ordinary individual human being must play the leading role in this Renaissance, and the battle he must fight is the struggle to transform his own life from within.

This, then, is the actual proof that the Nichiren Shoshu believer seeks in his or her own life—a victory in the battle for human revolution. A Buddhist practices faith with the awareness that, because of the oneness of life with the universe around it, a victory at a personal level will assure victory in the quest for *kosen-rufu*. This will be the greatest actual proof of all, for, as Nichiren Daishonin so poetically put it:

"In that time because all people chant Nam-myoho-renge-kyo together, the wind will not beleaguer the branches or boughs, nor will the rain fall hard enough to break a clod. . . . Disasters will be driven from the land, and the people will be rid of misfortune. They will also learn the way of living long, fulfilling lives. Realize that the time will come when the truth will be revealed that both the Person and the Law are unaging and eternal. There cannot be the slightest doubt about the sutra's solemn promise of a peaceful life in this world."

REFERENCES

Dialogue on Life, vol. 2. Daisaku Ikeda, Yoichi Kawada and Masahiro Kitagawa. Tokyo: Nichiren Shoshu International Center, 1977.

Outline of Buddhism. Yasuji Kirimura, ed. Tokyo: Nichiren Shoshu International Center, 1981.

Selected Lectures on the Gosho. Daisaku Ikeda. Tokyo: Nichiren Shoshu International Center, 1979.

SGI President Daisaku Ikeda discusses principles of Buddhist practice with NSA members in Santa Monica, California.

5
An Overview of the SGI

A History of the Soka Gakkai International

At a meeting in Guam in 1975, representatives of some fifty-one nations gathered to create the Soka Gakkai International (SGI), an umbrella organization for all Nichiren Shoshu Buddhist lay organizations throughout the world. As the years have passed, this organization has taken on added significance as the international movement itself has gained momentum. Daisaku Ikeda, third president of the Soka Gakkai lay organization in Japan and now Soka Gakkai International president, has in the past few years traveled extensively throughout the world under the aegis of the SGI to carry the Buddhist message of peace and hope to troubled peoples.

True Buddhism began in Japan. Nichiren Daishonin was the founder of the religion, and several centuries later, in 1930, a Japanese educator named Tsunesaburo Makiguchi formed a lay organization based on faith in Nichiren Daishonin's teachings. That organization is now known as the Soka Gakkai, which has a membership of some ten million and which works in concert with the Nichiren Shoshu priesthood to carry out the will of the Daishonin.

During World War II, however, Mr. Makiguchi was thrown in prison where he died for his pacifistic beliefs. After being released from his own wrongful imprisonment, his disciple, Josei Toda, took over the reins of the organization. By the time of his death in 1958, Toda had fostered the Soka Gakkai into a unified, nationwide network of more than 700,000 people. It was up to Toda's closest disciple, Daisaku Ikeda, to oversee the subsequent development of the organization. In 1975, Mr. Ikeda assumed leadership of the SGI in addition to his responsibilities for the Soka Gakkai, and in 1979, largely to devote himself to the global movement, he resigned as third president of the Soka Gakkai, retaining the title of honorary president.

It was only natural that Mr. Ikeda would become the driving force for the worldwide movement, for he had been the one who first had journeyed abroad to foster lay organizations in countries outside Japan. In 1960, he made his initial trip, visiting North and South America. As a result, NSA (Nichiren Shoshu Soka Gakkai of America) was created, along with organizations in Brazil and Canada. Further journeys consolidated the lay movement in other countries.

In addition to his efforts to aid the formation of lay organizations, Mr. Ikeda has met with heads of government and cultural leaders in nations across the globe. He has been to the Soviet Union and China on several occasions and has hosted foreign dignitaries on their visits to Japan. And it is to Daisaku Ikeda the man and his dream—to establish harmony and mutual understanding among all the peoples of the world—that the next section is devoted.

Profile of Daisaku Ikeda

More than anything else, Daisaku Ikeda, president of the Soka Gakkai International and honorary president of the Soka Gakkai, is a man of peace. His thinking starts from the principle that war is absolutely impermissible, and that military preparedness, far from being a deterrent to war, actually poses the risk of a holocaust that could wipe humanity from the face of the earth. To his mind, the fundamental requisite for permanent world peace is mutual understanding and friendship between peoples of the various nations of the world. By this, he does not mean just political or economic agreements, though these are desirable; instead, he envisions friendships among the common people of the world that link them heart to heart in a mutual quest for peace, prosperity and happiness—friendships that bridge all national, racial and ideological boundaries.

Born in 1928, Mr. Ikeda was only nine when the Sino-Japanese War began. He did not actually serve during World War II, but two of his most vivid recollections are connected with that war. One is the news of his brother's death on the battlefield, and the other is the look of grief on his mother's face when she learned that her eldest son had been killed. His attitude is succinctly stated in the opening of his eleven-volume (and still uncompleted) history of the Soka Gakkai, *The Human Revolution:* "War is barbarous and inhuman. Nothing is more cruel, nothing more tragic."

Mr. Ikeda is by no means uninterested in political or economic relations among nations, but he feels that the truly important task today is to develop international exchanges in the fields of education and culture. In his journeys to the United States, China, the Soviet Union, India and the various countries of Asia, Western Europe, Central and South America, he has tried diligently to find points of mutual interest and agreement that can serve as a basis for closer ties at the popular level.

As the founder of Soka University near Tokyo, he is vitally concerned with the exchange of ideas, as well as the exchange of students and professors, between universities in different countries. In the past few years, he has visited more than twenty major universities, including Oxford, Cambridge, the University of Paris, Columbia, the University of Chicago, the University of California at Berkeley and Los Angeles, Beijing University, Fudan University, Universidad Nacional Mayor de San Marcos de Lima, Moscow State University, University of Delhi, Jawaharlal Nehru University and Sofia State University. At each of these centers of learning, he has not only held discussions with administrative and faculty members but also had opportunities to associate with the students and question them directly about their lives, opinions and ambitions.

Mr. Ikeda likes people and he makes himself at home wherever he goes, whether it be Denver, Colorado, or Lima, Peru. He has been made an honorary citizen of forty-nine foreign cities, many of which have given him citations of merit. The fifty-four-year-old ambassador of goodwill thinks of himself not as an ideologue, but primarily as one human being working for peace. To him, people are more important than ideology. He is acutely aware that whatever a person might believe, he is still a human being deserving of respect.

In that connection, he has repeatedly stressed working together with the common people of the world. At the Soka Gakkai's Thirty-ninth General Meeting on October 24, 1976, he established the following five points as the fixed and unchanging definition of the Soka Gakkai spirit:

- That the Soka Gakkai shall forever stand on the side of the common people of the world.
- That the Soka Gakkai shall devote itself to carrying out the movement for human revolution.
- That the Soka Gakkai shall forever walk the great Middle Way of Buddhism.
- That the social aim of the Soka Gakkai shall be to preserve peace and to work for the advancement of true human culture.
- That the Soka Gakkai shall guard to the end the freedom of the human spirit, and in particular the principle of religious freedom.

As the leader of a great Buddhist lay organization, Mr. Ikeda is a diligent teacher and student of Buddhist philosophy, in particular, the philosophy of life and compassion handed down by Nichiren Daishonin. Indeed, his every thought and act is founded on Buddhism, which he regards as the sole true religion for peace, but he does not seek to impose his faith on others. He believes, as the Buddhism of Nichiren Daishonin teaches, that each single life is of the utmost importance, and that our prime duty is to respect and protect the right of each person to live.

As a nineteen-year-old, Daisaku Ikeda joined the Soka Gakkai in August 1947, during a period when Japan was in the throes of defeat and despair. The turning point for Mr. Ikeda came when he met Josei Toda, who during the war had been imprisoned for two years because of his opposition to the Japanese military establishment, and who was then reorganizing the Soka Gakkai. Young Daisaku was so impressed by Mr. Toda's faith and character that he became a loyal and active disciple. He still speaks of Mr. Toda as "my teacher in life." He studied under Mr. Toda for the next eleven years, succeeding to the presidency of the Soka Gakkai on May 3, 1960, two years after his mentor's passing.

Mr. Ikeda is a prolific writer and poet, and he is a great admirer of the poetry of Walt Whitman. Using the Japanese *haiku* style of poetry, Mr. Ikeda will dash off a poem on the spot to encourage and praise someone he has met. His continuing work, *The Human Revolution,* uses a novel format to tell the tale of the Soka Gakkai's vast movement for peace and culture. Each volume has sold more than one million copies.

In his writings, Mr. Ikeda thoroughly elucidates his belief that permanent world peace can be achieved only if nations subordinate their individual interests to the common cause of mankind. In volume four of *The Human Revolution,* he proposed a world summit conference for the abolition of nuclear weapons, and in volume five, he recommended that Japan attempt to make treaties of peace with every country, particularly the People's Republic of China.

He has continually stressed that Buddhists have a sacred duty to work for world peace. In an address delivered at the Thirty-fifth General Meeting of the Soka Gakkai on November 2, 1972, he said:

> The most horrible of war's aspects is probably not the cruelty and evil of its effects, but the fact that it brings to the forefront the vilest, most atrocious elements of the human life-force. War strips nobility and respect from humanity, and, through its wicked actions, covers man with filth. It is only natural that Buddhism, the aim of which is to guide all people to the highest, purest realms, is bound to engage in direct combat with war. By a like token, the Buddhist believer who is eager to practice his faith in the truest way regards it as his mission to pour his entire soul into the task of building peace.

Mr. Ikeda strongly believes that the United Nations should be accorded far greater powers than it now possesses. He feels the U.N. is impotent because it lacks the strength to impose its decisions on the two superpowers, the United States and the Soviet Union. In Hawaii in August 1981, Mr. Ikeda presided over the second annual general meeting of the Soka Gakkai International, and he again took up the theme of nuclear weaponry and the United Nations' role in world peace. He said:

> Recent arguments over how to wage a first strike to gain victory obviously imply the framing of strategic programs in which nuclear weapons are no longer thought to be "unusable" but "usable." The recently introduced neutron bomb, which is frowned upon by those who desire peace, is capable of instantaneously annihilating man without devastating buildings, is only an extension of the same old argument—an inevitable product of an argument based upon distrust, hatred and fear. For this reason, do you not agree that ours is the very age which requires a strenuous effort to unveil the essential evil of nuclear weapons?

> Although I feel that the United Nations is still too ridden with defects and faults to further advance toward peace, I would nonetheless like to ask all of you, for the sake of world peace, to strengthen your support for this organization, respecting its spirit as defined in its charter, and to launch a promotional and informational campaign to bolster and enhance the United Nations so that it can be an effective vehicle for perpetual peace on this planet.

The Soka Gakkai was founded on Tsunesaburo Makiguchi's system of value-creating education, and in the nineteen years of Mr. Ikeda's tenure as president (he resigned in 1979 to devote himself to the Soka Gakkai International, retaining the title of honorary president of the Soka Gakkai), the organization put considerable effort into the cause of liberal education. Soka University, which he founded along with several elementary, junior high and senior high schools, has placed itself at the forefront of this movement.

Mr. Ikeda has even conceived of a United Nations for Education, which would operate as a thoroughly non-political conference of educators, student representatives, parents' representatives and cultural leaders from all over the world, functioning to promote educational exchange, to provide financial aid or technical aid where needed, and in general to fulfill the purposes for which UNESCO was established. He has proposed to a number of foreign educators that a beginning could be made by establishing an International Conference of University Presidents and an International Conference of Student Representatives.

He is a great believer in the need for personal dialogues between leaders from different cultural areas.

Particularly noteworthy were his extended conversations with the late Dr. Toynbee in London in 1972 and 1973, which covered topics ranging from the human being as a social animal to the nature of life and the role of religion in the modern world. These dialogues have been published in book form in Japanese (1975), English (1976), Spanish (1980) and French (1981).

Mr. Ikeda has resolved to spend as much time as possible traveling to various countries in the interest of peace and international goodwill; he has made more than thirty overseas trips, visiting some forty nations. Traveling to different countries gives him the opportunity to engage in which he calls "human diplomacy," by which he means person-to-person diplomacy. Wherever he goes, he talks not only with political and cultural leaders, but with as many of the ordinary people as possible. Fundamentally, he believes that the most important people are the ordinary people.

In the world today, it would be difficult to find a person who has devoted so much time and sincerity to the cause of world peace. "If I can contribute even in a small way to the achievement of permanent peace," he says, "I shall be happy to travel here and there about the world for the rest of my life."

In sum, Daisaku Ikeda is, more than anything else, a man committed to peace.

NSA members practice the recitation of gongyo together at one of the nightly gatherings. Gongyo is the foundation of the practice of true Buddhism.

A discussion meeting, at which guests are introduced to the practice of orthodox Buddhism, is always a happy occasion.

NSA members hold a parade through the heart of Waikiki, part of an ongoing celebration of the human spirit which reveals itself in civic and cultural events, as well as in the participants' personal lives.

NSA members gather in Philadelphia on July 4, 1987, to celebrate the bicentennial of the nation's Constitution. Members, wherever they practice, always work for the betterment of their society, while saluting its heritage.

A sign of the growth in the number of people who believe in Nichiren Daishonin's Buddhism is exhibited at the larger scale gatherings hosted by NSA.

Throughout the spring and summer of 1987, NSA sponsored a tour of the New Freedom Bell throughout the United States. This replica of the original Liberty Bell served as the primary national effort to mark the bicentennial of the U.S. Constitution. The bell traveled 11,500 miles to 44 cities.

Buddhism's universal appeal has attracted people from all walks of life. Here, famous jazz musicians, including Herbie Hancock and Buster Williams—all members of NSA—perform at the SGI World Peace Youth Culture Festival.

Nichiren Daishonin's Buddhism is introduced to Americans at discussion meetings held voluntarily in the homes of members.

Youthful members of NSA exhibit the enthusiasm they gain from practicing Buddhism. NSA members are dedicated to sharing this enthusiasm with others.

The young men of NSA show the enthusiasm and joy they have gained through their practice of Buddhism by constructing a human ladder-tower.

Each year the Soka Gakkai International hosts a World Peace Youth Culture Festival with participants from countries throughout the world. The festivals abound with expressions of human vitality and camaraderie.

Starting as only a handful of believers, NSA has blossomed into an energetic and massive movement for human and cultural rejuvenation.

NSA cultural events bring Buddhism to life.

6

NSA—The American Buddhist Movement

History of NSA

The Buddhism of Nichiren Daishonin made its way to America in the hearts and minds of the wives of American servicemen returning from overseas duty in Japan. Scattered throughout the United States, these few war bride believers had little or no contact with each other until a man named Masayasu Sadanaga came here in 1957. He took it upon himself to encourage them and to establish an informal network of communication so that others, too, might take up the faith. Later, he became a naturalized American and took the name George M. Williams. To this day he considers himself a native American, and he shows his love for his "homeland" by spreading what he considers the fundamental means to people's happiness—faith in true Buddhism.

The organization of lay believers now known as NSA (Nichiren Shoshu Soka Gakkai of America) was officially formed in 1960 during a visit by Daisaku Ikeda, then president of the Soka Gakkai, Japan's lay organization, and now president of the global Soka Gakkai International. Mr. Williams personally took up the challenge of spearheading the organization and spurring its growth from few to many thousands. Today, he holds the post of general director of NSA, as well as the position of vice president of the Soka Gakkai International. NSA is a legally recognized nonprofit religious corporation in all fifty states.

In 1967, in recognition of the growth of the membership in America, the Nichiren Shoshu priesthood built its first overseas temple here on American soil. Myoho-ji Temple near Etiwanda, California, about fifty miles east of Los Angeles, was officially opened in a ceremony attended by President Ikeda, Mr. Williams and scores of members, and conducted by the sixty-sixth high priest of Nichiren Shoshu, Nittatsu Shonin. Since then, the priesthood and laity in the United States have striven together to help the American public learn of the Buddhism of Nichiren Daishonin.

The basic emphasis of NSA has always been on the introduction of people to the Buddhist faith. This is done so that people can, through the practice of Nichiren Shoshu Buddhism, carry out their own self-reformation, a self-reformation that will lay the foundation for world peace. The goal of introducing others is accomplished through the NSA discussion meeting, a gathering in people's homes throughout the country where invited guests can come and air their problems, seek the answers that Buddhism offers, and hear from those who already believe in Buddhism tales of their human revolution and benefits from practicing. Quite appropriately, these discussion meetings have come to be known as people's forums, because nowhere else can people of so many diverse backgrounds, nationalities and beliefs gather in a single meeting of the heart.

NSA also conducts study programs so members can come to grasp the essence of the truths of Buddhism and thereby apply them to their daily lives according to the prescription, "faith equals daily life."

NSA has long been active in the cultural-civic field as well. Its brass band and fife and drum corps marching units routinely appear in some of the nation's biggest parades, including the Columbus Day Parade in Chicago, the Cherry Blossom Parade in Washington, D.C., and the Mother Goose Parade in San Diego. In recognition of the nation's bicentennial, NSA sponsored a huge celebration in New York, Boston and Philadelphia in 1976. Parades, shows and meetings extolled the country's 200-year tradition of freedom. In 1987, NSA sponsored a nationwide tour of a replica of the Liberty Bell, called the New Freedom Bell, to salute the bicentennial of the U.S. Constitution.

Mr. Williams himself has been active through the years in bringing the teachings of Buddhism to American youth through a series of college and university seminars at more than eighty campuses. Some of the schools he has visited include: Harvard, Stanford, Princeton, Berkeley, the U.S. Air Force Academy, Rice,

UCLA, the City University of New York, the University of Colorado, the University of Nebraska, the University of New Mexico, the University of Maryland, the University of Southern California, the University of Hawaii, Oberlin College, the University of Illinois, Memphis State University, Boston University, Cornell University and many others.

Presently, NSA maintains community centers in most all major cities in the United States. At these locales, members can gather for larger, area-wide meetings to augment the smaller, ongoing discussion meetings. The national headquarters by NSA is in Santa Monica, California, and it is in this building, which is also called the World Culture Center, where a special Gohonzon inscribed specifically for "the attainment of the great desire for world peace and kosen-rufu" is enshrined. This special Gohonzon was bestowed on NSA by the sixty-seventh high priest of Nichiren Shoshu, Nikken Shonin, in recognition of America's central role in spreading Buddhism far and wide.

But most of all, NSA is people, and you will find NSA members in virtually every field of endeavor in society. There are doctors, lawyers, actors, students, teachers, servicemen and women, writers, artists, career women, housewives, skilled laborers, musicians, dancers, photographers, sales representatives, store owners and many others. Indeed, wherever you find an NSA member, you are sure to find a little bit of NSA in the hope, joy and confidence that that person exudes.

Background of George M. Williams

The current general director of NSA, George M. Williams, was born in Seoul, Korea of Japanese parents in 1930. After the Second World War, he moved with his parents to Japan, and in 1953 he took up faith in true Buddhism along with his mother. As a student and youthful believer, he was active in the Soka Gakkai under its second president, Josei Toda, and his disciple, Daisaku Ikeda. He learned much of his vast knowledge of Buddhism from these two and their lectures and guidance.

After graduating from Meiji University with a degree in law, Mr. Williams (who, as previously mentioned, was then named Masa-yasu Sadanaga) came to the United States to further his studies. This was in 1957. Sensing in Mr. Toda's words at his departure, "Don't try to spread Buddhism, just study hard," a subtle hint to actually do both, Mr. Williams began dedicating his whole life to the cause of introducing Buddhism to the American people. He has not wavered in his dedication since those struggling days as a student at UCLA and later at George Washington University and the University of Maryland. Despite the difficulty of learning a new language, Mr. Williams received a master's degree in political science in 1962. It should be noted that all through this period of his American education, he was busily involved in laying the groundwork for NSA.

Having been a Methodist himself when his mother urged him to join Nichiren Shoshu, Mr. Williams understands full well the difficulties that Westerners face in taking up an Eastern religion. In his own case, however, he found that Nichiren Daishonin's Buddhism soon cleared up the many misconceptions that he harbored about life. He now believes the American people, too, can find in this Buddhism the solution to their most vexing problems and the answer to the riddle of life that they cannot solve with any other religion or philosophy.

In his capacity as the leader of NSA, Mr. Williams has traveled throughout the United States on repeated occasions to take the message of Nichiren Shoshu Buddhism wherever there is a receptive ear. On his travels he meets constantly with the members of NSA. He attends their meetings to share his experience and impart the lessons in faith he has learned, and he struggles side by side with them in their quest to show others the truth and beauty of this religion.

In a recent article in the NSA newspaper, the *World Tribune,* which he founded and now edits and publishes, he wrote:

Buddhism is humanism. It teaches that every individual has the right to become happy. Human freedom, equality, respect for the dignity of human life—these have long been advocated, but where are these today? Neither political change nor greater awareness gained from academic scholarship alone can guarantee happiness.

Seven hundred years ago, Nichiren Daishonin stood alone and had great compassion to share the kind of true happiness which would enable each individual to live a life of joy no matter how cruel or painful their world became. Based on this same spirit, we in NSA are also determined to work for this cause with the great Buddhist teaching he left us.

And, it can be said, devotion to a grand cause is the prime motivating factor of this man who is championing the Buddhist teaching in America, a man to whom thousands of people are grateful for the new lives they forged through faith in true Buddhism.

While saluting all that is good about their country, NSA members strive to usher in a new age of humanistic and life-affirming principles.

Appendix I
Toward the 21st Century

In his first university lecture outside of Japan, SGI President Daisaku Ikeda spoke to 500 UCLA students on April 1, 1974. The talk summarized the challenges facing mankind in the decades ahead. Mr. Ikeda emphasized the need for an understanding of life and the exercise of humanism in all of man's affairs.

I am very pleased to have been invited to speak here today at the University of California, Los Angeles. I would like to express my sincere appreciation to the Chancellor, Dr. Young, Vice-Chancellor Miller and all of the students and faculty who are attending this afternoon. I would like to talk with you, not as a formal lecturer, but as a friend who is deeply concerned with your future development. You are the people who will soon shoulder the responsibility of leadership for the future—not just for America, but for the entire world in the twenty-first century. Your time is coming very soon. In twenty-five years, your generation must face the many challenges that lie ahead.

During the past two years, I have had the opportunity to hold many life-to-life dialogues with Dr. Arnold Toynbee, the renowned English philosopher and historian. We met in England during the spring of 1972 and 1973, and I felt that our ten days together were extremely productive. The value of this type of person-to-person communication is that it mutually inspires each participant.

Dr. Toynbee is one of the greatest men of our time. He has an extremely sharp mind and, although he is eighty-five years old, is still a man in the prime of life. He has never stopped his creative work.

Dr. and Mrs. Toynbee wake up at six o'clock each morning, while most of us are still in bed. The Toynbees, meanwhile, are cleaning up their room and then eating breakfast. At nine o'clock,

Dr. Toynbee enters the study, sits down at his desk and begins to work. From his example, I can truly understand the gracefulness of aging. There is certainly beauty in youth, yet, there is a different, noble quality in those who have aged beautifully.

During our talks, I asked Dr. Toynbee if he had any special motto for his life. He simply mentioned the Latin work, "Laboramus"—which means, "Now let's work." These same words were spoken by the Roman Emperor Severus as he lay on his deathbed during a campaign in North England in 211 A.D. It was cold and desolate, and he was dying, but he continued to take command from his bed. Just before he died, he uttered this motto, "Now let's work" to his troops. As Dr. Toynbee was telling me this story, I realized that this simple motto was the real secret to his vigorous health and youthful manner. I was able to see the true beauty of any man who carries on a lifelong struggle in pursuit of a great ideal.

Our talks covered a wide range of subject matter. We discussed civilization, study, education, literature, art, the nature of life, the natural sciences, international affairs, social problems, ethics and the new role of women. Our discussions went on and on as we probed ever deeper into the twenty-first century. All in all, these conversations lasted more than forty hours. Even after I returned to Japan, we continued our dialogue through innumerable letters.

I remember my first meeting with Dr. Toynbee. He had a very solemn expression, and, with a determined voice, said, "For the sake of all mankind in the twenty-first century, let's proceed." He shared a profound concern for the world to come after his life is over. His deep compassion was genuine and moving, and I could not help but be impressed by it. On several occasions, he expressed his strong desire to be able to leave a message for all of us, the younger generation. I must confess I feel the same sincere need to pass on something of value today to all of you.

Walking the path of the 'Golden Mean'

As we neared the conclusion of our discussions, I asked Dr. Toynbee what he foresaw for mankind in the twenty-first century. He replied, "Man in the twentieth century has become intoxicated by the power of technology. However, this same technology has poisoned our environment and led the human race toward self-destruction. Man must gain the wisdom to examine and control himself. Therefore, we must be very cautious about the extremes of self-indulgence on one hand and the suppression of the will on the other. We must walk the path of the 'Golden Mean.' Mankind must progress along a middle path."

I found myself in complete agreement with Dr. Toynbee's evaluation. I was especially impressed by his use of the term, "Golden Mean." Mahayana Buddhism, which is the essence of Oriental philosophy, is based on the fundamental principle which Dr. Toynbee described as the "Golden Mean."

Much of Western thought seems to have been directed toward either spiritualism or materialism. Communist countries tend toward a society whose primary goals are material in nature; so-called Western nations, having a Christian background, speak of the only "true values" as being spiritual. I am convinced, however, that there is a third, or middle path, which can encompass both the extremes of spiritualism and those of cold materialism. The concept I am proposing is thoroughly described by Buddhism.

Dr. Toynbee and I also attempted to discuss concrete measures which would put our civilization back on the right track, but we soon realized that mere methodology or abstract theory alone are not sufficient. We both keenly felt that we had to address ourselves first to the basic root of all issues—namely, what is man, and what meaning does life hold for man? The nature of a human being, then, became the prime point of our talks.

To talk about a human being, or human activity, we both felt we had to clarify and examine the one common denominator of all mankind—life itself! It would be impossible to meaningfully discuss any human question until we had come to a basic understanding of life.

Dr. Toynbee has lived through two world wars, and he strongly asserted that there can be absolutely no justification for war. After experiencing the deep anguish of losing his own son in war, he was forced to re-examine the meaning life has to a human being, especially in terms of life and death.

I lost my own brother in the war. I, too, understand its great sufferings. There is *nothing* more barbarous or more miserable than war. As long as I live, I will speak out against war. My feelings about this will never change.

Recognizing the dignity of life

After sharing our experiences, we readily agreed that the most urgent task facing us today is to instill in the hearts of all mankind a genuine and lasting respect for the sanctity and dignity of life. I firmly believe that the primary concern of the twenty-first century should be the study, understanding and practice of true humanism, or exercising the recognition of the supreme dignity of life. Out of our present civilization of cold technology must rise a new civilization of humanism, with the issue of life squarely in the spotlight.

As we continued to discuss this weighty issue, a wide variety of related topics were covered. We talked about the relationship between spirit and matter, the eternity of life, the death penalty, euthanasia and egoism. Today, therefore, I would like to take the opportunity of examining the future of mankind from the viewpoint of a humanistic life-philosophy.

As many of you may already know, Buddhism describes our life as an accumulation of various sufferings. These sufferings have been basically categorized within the timeless cycle of birth, growing old, sickness and death. There are other types of sufferings, also, such as losing our loved ones, or not being able to satisfy your desires. Put very simply, Buddhism says that life is full of problems.

Sometimes we feel so happy that time itself seems to fly by. We want to hold this feeling forever, yet our joy inevitably fades away. As we watch these transient feelings of happiness slowly drift away, we begin to feel sorrow. The thought that we were so happy only a moment ago makes our sorrow even greater. Even time seems to slow down. Sufferings always seem to drag on. There are so many sufferings in this world. The situation of being poor in a rich world, the barriers of color and race, of nationality and culture—all add to man's suffering and anguish.

The Principle of Impermanence

Why, then do people suffer? Buddhism responds to this age-old problem by clearly explaining that people suffer because they are not **aware** of the impermanence of all things. Nothing is permanent, neither material things, nor any phenomena.

People experience sufferings because they do not recognize or refuse to accept this transiency.

It is a natural law that the young must grow old. It is also natural that anything with a physical form must ultimately deteriorate. The healthy will eventually become sick. All living things must die. Heraclitus stated that, "You cannot step twice into the same river, for fresh waters are ever flowing in upon you."

It looks as if this table, or this microphone, or even this building, are solidly constructed, but they will all crumble some day. If this had already happened, I wouldn't be here lecturing today. But I'm glad I didn't have to wait for that to happen. I'm afraid my body wouldn't last that long.

Buddhism clearly explains that suffering emerges in our hearts because we forget the principle of impermanence and believe that what we possess will last forever. Suppose you have a beautiful girlfriend. Do you ever go out on a date wondering what she will look like in thirty or forty years? I'm sure you don't. It is human nature to feel that the health and youth we have today will last forever.

By the same token, there are very few wealthy people who can imagine that their wealth will some day be exhausted and that they should work a little harder now. The wealthy man who is working hard is doing so only to gain a little more for immediate needs.

There's nothing wrong with people acting in this way. It is a perfectly natural human reaction. Nevertheless, we suffer because we have such notions. If you want to keep your sweetheart forever, you will have to struggle. And when you must leave a loved one, you will feel the deepest pain. Because men want to accumulate wealth, they will fight with their neighbors, and when they lose that wealth, they must taste the bitter fruit of suffering.

The prevailing concept of death follows the same pattern. We are alive now—it is an undeniable fact, and we don't go around thinking about death all the time. Unknowingly, we act as if our lives will last forever, and we make every possible effort to survive.

However, it is also undeniable that this attachment to life leads to all sorts of human suffering. Because we fear death, we are afraid of becoming old or sick and continue to struggle through the endless swamp of worldly desire. This is life's pattern.

Buddhism teaches us that we should clearly recognize these cycles of impermanence and have the courage to accept them. Instead of trying to escape from the inevitable decline facing all mortals, we can actually open the road to true *enlightenment* by accepting these laws of life.

Desires: life's motivating force

Buddhism has generally been regarded as a religion which requires the individual to abandon all worldly desires. It has been considered a hindrance to the prosperity of society and opposed to the advance of civilization. It is common knowledge that Buddhist countries are inferior to non-Buddhist ones in the development of scientific technology. Japan seems to be the only exception. However, this is not because she bases her ideology on Buddhism, but because she has skillfully adopted Western technology. Whatever the case, the lack of scientific development in Buddhist cultures cannot justly be attributed to Buddhism.

True Buddhism does not require the suppression of human desires. True Buddhism is not a passive or nihilistic religion. It is a teaching which clarifies that the source of all desire is life itself. In other words, true Buddhism reveals the eternal law which governs and harmonizes all phenomena in the universe.

Because life is impermanent, all flesh is mortal, and sufferings are inherent. However, Buddhism teaches us not to fear death but to grasp that which lies beyond mortality.

As I stated before, we cannot say that it is stupid to be charmed by fleeting pleasures, or swayed by worldly desires. No. As long as life continues, it is instinctual to want to live, to cherish love and to seek profit.

A life dominated by desire or swayed by external influences is only a superficial expression of the human ego. *Enlightenment* or awareness of the universal truth underlying all phenomena brings out the most noble and rewarding ego.

This highest ego is the fundamental principle of the universe. It is also the same law which controls the expression of the self within each individual. In my discussions with Dr. Toynbee, I learned that he referred to this ego as the "ultimate spiritual entity of the universe." He said we should try to understand this entity in terms of a universal "law," as Buddhism does rather than as a personification as many faiths in the West do.

Pursuing this true ego does not imply giving up a lesser or more superficial one. The fact is that the highest ego gives new direction to the lesser one.

Civilization advances because of the instincts and desires of men. The pursuit of wealth enables economic growth. The will to defy the winter cold led to the development of natural science. Somehow, love, which is a desire, inspired literature.

Some schools of Buddhism teach the suppression of all earthly desire. Because they equate desires with the mortal flesh, they even condone self-immolation. However, desires arise from the innermost core of life. They are absolutely indestructible. They are the motivating force behind all behavior.

So, it is absolutely necessary to give direction to the superficial ego. This ego is only meaningful when based on the loftier one. True Buddhism has clarified this highest ego as true human nature. I feel very strongly that our civilization will be able to make meaningful progress only if we understand this point.

Essence of life and death

Buddhism first encouraged individuals to recognize impermanence and to understand death. This was done to make them aware of the stark reality of the never-changing law of the universe. A Buddha is not someone who encourages escapism, but a common mortal innately enlightened to this law. In this state, he can ponder his own death and see the supreme Law running beneath the suface, because he knows that a man's life is a noble manifestation of the law itself.

Death is inevitable. No one can escape it But, Buddhism explains that death is only one expression of the endless cycle of life—birth, growth, maturity and death. Thus Buddhism urges us to have absolute belief in this principle, so that we may clearly perceive all phenomena, including death.

Buddhism expounds the oneness of life and death. That is, being alive or being dead are simply different expressions of the same life. There is a Buddhist term, *Ku,* which explains this. *Ku* is a concept that is neither existence nor non-existence. Dr. Toynbee agreed with me that the ultimate spiritual existence could only be grasped in terms of *Ku.*

It would be very difficult to explain *Ku* in a short time, but briefly, it does not mean void or nothingness as many people mistakenly believe. Existence and non-existence are restricted to the limitations of time and space. *Ku* is a concept beyond time and space. I am talking now about something that lies beyond the realm of existence and non-existence.

Let me explain further. As we grow older, we undergo tremendous change, both physically and mentally. You must have looked quite different when you were younger. During the long course of your life, you will change drastically in many ways. Yet, in each stage of growth, you always have the same self. It remains constant. This self, which retains its individuality forever, is called *Ga,* or self-identity, in Buddhism.

This self-identity shapes both your mind and your body. But self-identity is hard to pinpoint. We have no choice but to refer to it as the essence of life which molds your mind and body, thus transcending both existence and non-existence.

True Buddhism explains that an individual's self-identity corresponds to the life of the universe. This identity assumes the form of either life or death and exists eternally. This, briefly, is the basic concept of the oneness of life and death. Regardless of any environmental influences, man's highest condition still corresponds to the life of the universe.

If we put modern civilization into proper perspective, couldn't we honestly say that men are slaves to their egos? Human desire has polluted nature. We are on the verge of exhausting our oil supplies. The giant industrial complex that is the backbone of our society is nothing but a manifestation of human desire. The colossal skyscrapers, high-speed transportation systems, artificial foods and nuclear weapons—all these are products of desire.

It is obvious that if we allow our desires to run rampant, they will surely lead to the destruction of the world. There is a growing tendency to distrust the reckless progress of civilization. Attention is finally being focused on man himself. It seems that mankind has finally taken the first step toward becoming human.

A person blinded by desire, seeking only self-gratification, is no better than an animal, regardless of his intelligence. A man can only claim the title of "human being" when he is actively searching for the ultimate way of life.

Dr. Toynbee regards superficial desire as "evil desire," and the desire resulting from the true human ego as the "desire for love." "For the sake of the twenty-first century," he said, "it is indispensable for each individual to scrutinize his own life and to be his own master."

Crossroads for the human race

We can expect rational, harmonious progress toward the twenty-first century only if our most noble desires lead us to the truth. With a lofty purpose in life, man can stand on his own for the first time in history, and modern society will be revitalized. Therefore, I wish to assert that the twenty-first century should be a "Century of Life."

Life and the universe will go on, just as the wheels of time continue to turn. But it makes a great difference whether we are bogged down in the quagmire of desire or rolling smoothly on the firm ground of *enlightenment*. Civilization can definitely make sound progress if we're on solid ground. The direction of the future depends solely on whether or not mankind can analyze itself and realize the eternal truths of life. We are at the turning point today.

The turn of the century will be an important crossroads for the human race. It will be a time when men will have to decide whether to become true humans or to remain mere animals. Truthfully speaking, man has thus far been a slave to his animalistic nature. In the philosophy of Nichiren Daishonin, taught 700 years ago, the phrase "talented animal" appears. This term takes on greater significance all the time. It refers to everybody. I'd rather like to urge you to look for your true independence as warm and noble human beings.

I, myself, have begun a journey of human revolution by practicing the true Buddhism of Nichiren Daishonin. I hope that each one of you young pioneers will set out on a lifelong quest for true freedom in this chaotic age. This is why I related these fragments of Buddhist wisdom today. It would be my greatest pleasure if my words today would be of some help in guiding your future.

I sincerely thank you very much.

Appendix II
NSA Statistical Information

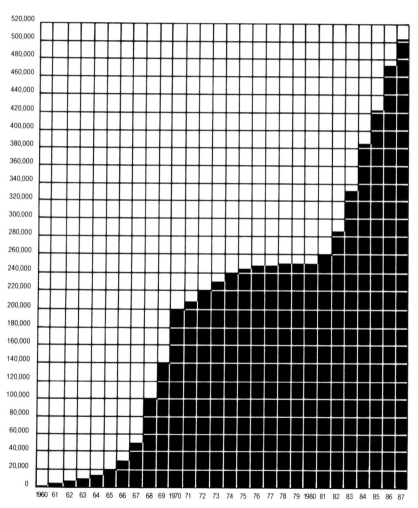

Figure 1. Growth in NSA membership, 1960-1987.

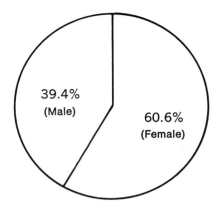

Figure 2. Sex distribution of NSA membership.

	25%	50%
Retired		
Homemaker		
Student		
Unskilled		
Skilled		
Sales		
Management		
Professional		
Service		
Unemployed		
Others		

Figure 3. Occupational distribution of NSA membership.

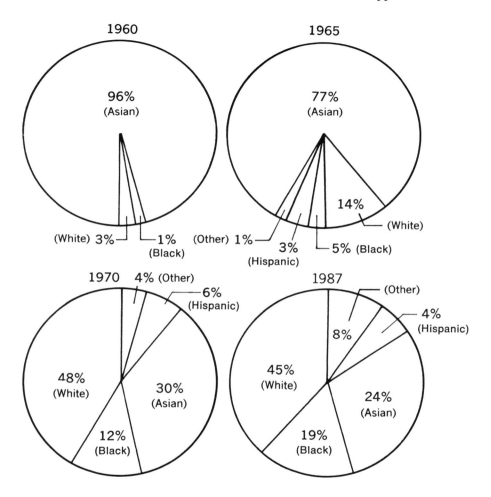

Figure 4. Changes in NSA's racial and ethnic distribution.

Appendix II

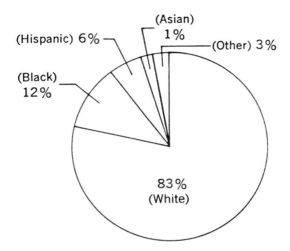

Figure 5. Racial and ethnic composition of the United States (1980 census).

Note: The total represents a figure over and above 100% of the population, since the U.S. census of 1980 did not include Hispanic as one of the categories in its ethnic and national origins categories; rather, it had a separate question asking individuals whether or not they had Hispanic origins. People with Hispanic backgrounds, then, had to make an additional choice on the ethnic and national origins question. About 40% of Hispanics chose the category of "other" indicating that they considered themselves primarily Hispanic, rather than either black or white. This is one of the factors making the "other" category rather large. In addition to Hispanics, the "other" category includes American Indians, Hawaiians, Eskimoes, Aleuts, Asian Indians, and other smaller groups.

Year \ Race	White	Black	Asian	Hispanic	Others	Total (%)
1950s	5.63	2.82	90.14	0.00	1.41	100.00
1960s	30.23	6.20	55.56	6.72	1.29	100.00
1970s	50.53	23.89	15.18	8.07	2.34	100.00
1980s	49.48	22.67	16.06	7.25	4.53	100.00
Average	45.07	19.61	25.14	7.27	2.90	100.00

Decade Joined

Figure 6. Racial distribution of respondents by decade joined.

Figure 7. Highest level of education attained by members surveyed.

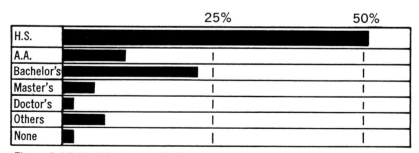

Figure 8. Highest degree received.

Appendix II

	25%	50%

Jewish	
Catholic	
Protestant*	
Islam	
Buddhist**	
Hindu	
Atheist	
Other	
None	

Figure 9. Previous religions of members surveyed.
 *Refer to Figure 10.
**Refer to Figure 11.

Lutheran	7.53%
Episcopalian	6.91%
Baptist	30.96%
Methodist	15.48%
Congregational	1.65%
Presbyterian	5.57%
Unitarian	1.34%
Others	13.62%
Not Specific	16.92%

Figure 10. Breakdown of Protestant sects to
which NSA members previously belonged.

Nichiren-shu sect	7.80%
Nembutsu sect	40.00%
Zen sect	6.83%
Shingon sect	7.80%
Others	8.78%
Not Specific	28.78%

Figure 11. Breakdown of other Buddhist sects
to which NSA members previously belonged.

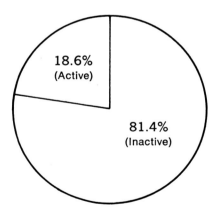

Figure 12. NSA members' level of partic-
ipation in their previous religions.

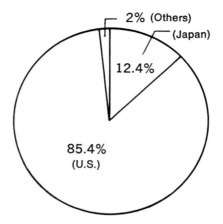

Figure 13. Country where members converted to Nichiren Shoshu.

	25%	50%
Friend		
Family		
Acquaintance		
Stranger		
Publication		
Other		

Figure 14. How respondents learned about Nichiren Shoshu.

Motivation	Frequency	
Finances	691	30.08%
Health	525	22.86%
Family	702	30.56%
Job	507	22.07%
Relationships	832	36.22%
Emotional growth	788	34.31%
Spiritual fulfillment	960	41.79%
Desire to contribute to society	496	21.59%
Desire for religious truth	746	32.48%
Others	268	11.67%
Total	6,515	

Figure 15. Motivation for joining NSA.

Appendix II

Motivation	1950	1960	1970	1980	Average
Finances	13.29	10.09	10.16	11.18	10.60
Health	22.38	13.12	6.70	7.17	8.14
Family	14.69	12.11	10.26	10.63	10.76
Job	4.20	6.28	7.56	8.59	7.70
Relationships	9.79	11.21	14.02	12.01	12.77
Emotional growth	8.39	9.30	12.95	12.30	12.09
Spiritual fulfillment	6.99	12.56	14.78	15.89	14.71
Desire to contribute to society	4.90	7.06	7.88	7.76	7.65
Desire for religious truth	7.69	11.10	11.64	11.55	11.44
Others	7.69	7.17	4.04	2.92	4.14
Total	100.00	100.00	100.00	100.00	100.00

Figure 16. Differences in reasons for joining according to decade (%).

Significant Benefits	Frequency	
Health	1,257	54.72%
Finances	1,391	60.56%
Relationships	1,572	68.44%
Family	1,507	65.61%
Job	1,379	60.03%
Emotional growth	1,798	78.28%
Spiritual development	1,637	71.27%
Others	185	8.05%
Total	10,716	

Figure 17. Significant benefits received through NSA practice.

Note: The selection of more than one item by the same person accounts for a total percentage which is well in excess of 100%. Numerical totals refer to number of survey respondents.

Greatest Benefits	Frequency	
Health	516	22.46%
Finances	330	14.37%
Relationships	819	35.66%
Family situation	683	29.73%
Job/Career	423	18.42%
Emotional growth	1,000	43.54%
Spiritual fulfillment	878	38.22%
Others	138	6.01%
Total	4,787	

Figure 18. Greatest benefit received since joining NSA.

Note: The selection of more than one item by the same person accounts for a total percentage which is well in excess of 100%. Numerical totals refer to number of survey respondents.